We Are All Multiculturalists Now

▲ ▲ ▲

Also by Nathan Glazer

The Lonely Crowd
(with David Riesman and Reuel Denney)

Faces in the Crowd
(with David Riesman)

American Judaism

Studies in Housing and Minority Groups
(Editor, with Davis McEntire)

The Social Basis of American Communism

Beyond the Melting Pot
(with Daniel P. Moynihan)

Remembering the Answers: Essays on the American Student Revolt

Ethnicity: Theory and Experience
(Editor, with Daniel P. Moynihan)

Affirmative Discrimination: Ethnic Inequality and Public Policy

The Urban Predicament
(Editor, with William Gorham)

Ethnic Pluralism and Public Policy
(Editor, with Ken Young)

Ethnic Dilemmas, 1964–1982

Clamor at the Gates: The New American Immigration
(Editor)

The Public Face of Architecture
(Editor, with Mark Lilla)

The Limits of Social Policy

Conflicting Images: India and the United States
(Editor, with Sulochana Raghavan Glazer)

We Are All Multiculturalists Now

▲ ▲ ▲

Nathan Glazer

HARVARD UNIVERSITY PRESS
Cambridge, Massachusetts
London, England
1997

Library of Congress Cataloging-in-Publication Data

Glazer, Nathan.
We are all multiculturalists now / Nathan Glazer.
p.   cm.
Includes bibliographical references and index.
ISBN 0-674-94851-3 (alk. paper)
1. Multicultural education—United States.
2. Multiculturalism—United States. I. Title
LC1099.3.G53   1997
370.117'0973—dc21   96-39900

CONTENTS

▲ ▲ ▲

"We are all socialists now," Sir William Harcourt was quoted as saying in 1889. He served as Chancellor of the Exchequer in the Cabinet of William Gladstone, and his best-known accomplishment was the imposition of a progressive tax on estates at death, to the outrage of owners of large estates. "We are all Keynesians now," President Richard Nixon is reputed to have said in 1971. *Omnia mutantur, nos et mutamur in illis* (All things change, and we change with them).

1 ▲▲▲▲▲▲▲▲▲▲▲▲▲▲▲▲▲

THE MULTICULTURAL
EXPLOSION

In May 1994 the *New York Times* published an inconspicuous item under the headline, "School Board Will Recognize Other Cultures, But as Inferior." Datelined Tavares, Florida—not one of the better-known locations in the state—the item reported that the conservative Christian members of the school board of Lake County, responding to a state-mandated program on teaching about other cultures, had passed a resolution declaring that "this instruction shall include and instill in our students an appreciation of our American heritage and culture such as: our republican form of government, capitalism, a free-enterprise system, patriotism, strong family values, freedom of religion and other basic values that are superior to other foreign or historic cultures."[1]

This was not an elegantly phrased statement, and it clearly reflected some annoyance at the state-mandated requirements, as well as some crudity in the school board members. But school boards reflect the people who elect them. The policy statement of the Lake County board had already stimulated a critical response: The teachers union said the policy violated the intent of the state law, passed in 1991, which declared, according to the *Times*, that students need to appreciate other cultures and "eliminate personal and national ethnocentrism so that they understand that a specific culture is not intrinsically superior or inferior to another." The teachers union threatened a law suit. The superintendent of schools was clearly going to be cautious in implementing the board policy: "There's a lot of unanswered questions about it . . . I guess according to the policy it could be one grade." (First grade, perhaps? First-graders probably all already believed in American superiority anyway.) The superintendent's office had been swamped with calls, half for and half against the new policy.

There was much to wonder about in this report, which was not explored either in this brief item or in a lengthier follow-up story on Lake County. One wondered, for example, why the Florida state legislature had passed this law in 1991 in the first place, and what had occasioned it. Could it have been a serious concern over student failure to appreciate foreign cultures, or was it rather concern over student failure to appreciate African American culture, or Hispanic or Cuban culture? Which legislators, of which groups, pressed for this action? One would have had to know who introduced the law, and why, and what the role of the state education department was in the making of the law in order to understand its intent. But one suspected that a concern over cultures inside the United States itself rather than outside it had occasioned the state legislative action. One wondered too if the policy statement of the Lake County school board should really be considered at odds with the state law: After all, the statement refers only to basic values and institutions which on the whole are not challenged in the United States, and asserts only that these values are superior to those we might find in other foreign or historic cultures.

One wondered most at the combativeness of the teachers of Lake County. This is not, after all, cosmopolitan Dade County. As the *Times* pointed out, it is an inland county, northwest of Orlando, attracting, alongside its remaining farmers, retirees who cannot afford to live on the expensive coasts, many of whom live in trailer courts.

In the follow-up story in the *Times*, one learned that the state Education Commissioner, Doug Jameson, "quickly condemned the new policy."[2] The chairman of People for Mainstream Values, a local political action group, was quoted as saying, "We are already teaching our children to love and honor our country, so why spend all this time and money talking about something we are already doing? We've become sort of a laughingstock." A history teacher was quoted as saying, "We regard American culture as very diverse, and we're not sure what values they see as American culture." (So much for republicanism, free enterprise, patriotism, strong family values, freedom of religion, and so on.)

A few months later, in a run-off election, members of the school board who had voted for the policy were defeated by opponents pledged to repeal it. "The losers asserted that the teachers unions and liberal news organizations were responsible for their defeat,"[3] but the voters may very well have been worried about their county becoming a laughingstock, an emblem of backwardness.

One can draw many and diverse lessons from this relatively minor battle in the culture wars. Perhaps there is no lesson to be drawn at all except that the voters of Lake County are split over whether they want persons identified with the Christian Coalition governing the local schools; and after having elected some in one election, they turned them out in another. Had the policy been proposed by a less divided and controversial board, perhaps there would have been no national story at all. But I find it revealing that in a rural and small-town county where the local team is called the Patriots and the school colors are red, white, and blue, this policy aroused the opposition it did, and attracted the national attention it did. Others have also found in the story something symbolic and representative of larger and questionable changes in the country, and they are given pause not so much by the action of the school board as by the strong reaction to it that led to its defeat.

It is not surprising that Lynne Cheney, the former head of the National Endowment for the Humanities and a leading critic of multicultural trends in education, was troubled. She wrote: "The original board action made an important point. There are, to be sure, many ways in which we are not superior to other cultures . . . Nonetheless, there are many in which we are the light of the world; and one of them is that we have created a single nation out of people from every part of the world."[4] It was rather more surprising that Todd Gitlin, a writer identified with the left, also found something noteworthy in the reaction to the action of the school board: "The truly remarkable thing—all the more remarkable for not being remarked on—was that this was a newsworthy story in the first place. Not so many decades ago, it would have been taken for granted that America was the pinnacle of civilizations."[5] While he is more ambivalent than Lynne Cheney, he does not applaud the widespread denunciation of the school board.

I too have drawn a lesson from this story, and from much else that is going on in American education. It is that multiculturalism in education—so strongly denounced by so many powerful voices in American life, by historians, publicists, labor leaders, intellectuals, the occasion for so many major battles in American education during the nineties, and so much at odds with the course of American culture, society, and education at least up until the 1960s—has, in a word, won. I do not assert this either to sound an alarm over this victory or to celebrate it. I feel warmly attached to the old America that was acclaimed in school textbooks and that is now passing—at least in the textbooks. Despite all its faults and errors and prejudices and, if you will, crimes, it did, after all, bring into its fold over time, though not without political conflict and even Civil War, the peoples and races it had rejected; it did offer them opportunities; it did correct its errors and faults and to some extent make reparation for the harm its laws and practices had imposed.

Nevertheless, many, among minorities and women in particular, have found all this wanting and inadequate. And those who complain about the practices and perspectives of the old America have been most successful in the sphere of education. Schools, the public schools in particular but also institutions of higher education, have long served to bring excluded groups into the common fold, by assimilating them to American culture, by teaching them the skills to enter the economy, by educating them about American politics and practices in many spheres of life. The schools continue to serve this function. But where once it was taken for granted that public education had as little reason to notice or help maintain separate minority group cultures among students as to notice or help maintain religion, of whatever kind, today a new dispensation prevails, and it will not change for a long time. That new dispensation, which is commonly summed up in the term "multiculturalism," and what has brought it about are the subjects of this book.

Most of the flood of literature on multiculturalism has dealt with higher education: with the fate of the old canon of great literature and its partial replacement by new canons, with the rise of ethnic and racial and women's studies, with the surprising changes in the aims and character of much scholarly research in history and literature, with the quality of life in higher education as it becomes increasingly responsive to the sensitivities of racial minorities and women and creates new rules and new programs to teach students and faculty and administrators how to properly respond and relate to minority and female students, faculty, and administrators. This is an important change, but I will not have much to say about it. A good deal has already been written by critics and defenders of these changes. The critics may sometimes exaggerate how this new concern for sensitivity to what are perceived as group slights or discrimination has affected the overall tone of life in higher education, and in the catalog of outrageous incidents they have developed to illustrate the new environment, the critics have undoubtedly got some of the facts wrong.[6] But there is indeed something distasteful in these developments overall. The fact that the charge of "political correctness" is so vigorously denied by defenders of this new censoriousness is an indication of its unattractiveness. The fact that the longest piece of literature an incoming professor may get to prepare him for his job is the guidelines on sexual harassment, as I have heard from one incoming professor, suggests imbalance at the least. (I have not researched the matter; he may have been exaggerating; and of course the incoming faculty member, in many fields, is now as likely to be female as male.)

If multiculturalism has established a powerful position in higher education, it is perhaps not so surprising. Higher education is devoted, we are all told, to pushing out frontiers in research and teaching. One gets ahead in academia by developing a new point of view, perhaps indeed an outrageous one. When one promotes this new point of view in literature or some other field of the humanities, or in some parts of the social sciences (such as anthropology), there is little constraint from an external world of experiments and facts and numbers to limit the unleashed mind. Indeed, so vulnerable is higher education in the humanities and social sciences to winds of fashion that in some respects multiculturalism may have already reached its high point, and we may see some recession. I sense that the pressure for required courses designed to expand students' knowledge of and sensitivity to minority cultures has been reduced, or the willingness to resist them has increased. But one should not expect any reduction overall in academic courses and programs reflecting new multicultural interests and sensitivities. In the humanities and social sciences, multiculturalism has established a solid beach-head that is expressed in the substantial number of offerings in these fields. In some new areas, such as gay and lesbian studies (which are now also encompassed, as are women's studies, under the capacious label of multiculturalism), one can only expect further expansion.

What is more surprising than these developments in higher education, however, is how complete has been the victory of multiculturalism in the public schools of America—even in those of Lake County, Florida, where, without further knowledge, we would have assumed the schools were fully rooted in the orientations of the old America and were less affected by the trends that are reshaping the schools of the central cities. The American public school, originally established to mold Americans of all backgrounds into a common culture and fully devoted to this task until perhaps two decades ago, has undergone a remarkable change in the last twenty years. The change had received almost no public notice as recently as a few years ago. But then came the multicultural explosion, in which conflict over how much we should change the common understanding of American history and society in the public schools broke out, first in California, then in New York, and eventually in school districts throughout the country. Multiculturalism has so solidly established itself in the public school curriculum that few would find it remarkable that a teacher in Lake County, Florida, could say today: "We regard American culture as very diverse, and we're not sure what values they see as American values."

Only very recently has the term "multiculturalism" been applied to these developments. The word has emerged and spread so rapidly, has been applied to so many phenomena in so many contexts, has been used in attack and in defense so often to cover such very different developments, that it is no easy task to describe what one means by multiculturalism. It is not in the spell-check dictionary of my word processor. The Nexis data base of major newspapers shows no references to multiculturalism as late as 1988, a mere 33 items in 1989, and only after that a rapid rise—more than 100 items in 1990, more than 600 in 1991, almost 900 in 1992, 1200 in 1993, and 1500 in 1994, the year of the Lake County battle. That may have been the peak year, but over 1200 references in 1995 demonstrate the vigor of the issue. Of course the drop in the number of newspaper references since 1994 may reflect the fact that in many respects multiculturalism in the schools is no longer news, but quotidian reality.

"Multiculturalism" is absent from the original *Oxford English Dictionary* but makes an appearance in the 1989 revised edition. Almost every example of its use there is from Canada (the very first is an oddity from the *New York Herald Tribune Books* of 1941). Almost every book in the Harvard University libraries listed as containing the word "multiculturalism" in its title in the 1970s and 1980s is Canadian or Australian. It makes sense that the word would come to us from our neighbor to the north. Canada has had to deal with two major languages and two cultures, but has also found it necessary or desirable to elevate minority European immigrant groups as a third element, entitled to share in Canadian multiculturalism. Australia, with less reason, has also been a pioneer in the use of the term and in the spread of multiculturalism in school programs and elsewhere.

But here in America, the word multiculturalism is a newcomer. James Banks, the most prolific writer of textbooks for teachers on multiculturalism and the editor of the massive 1995 *Handbook of Research on Multicultural Education,* used the term "multiethnic" education in his early books and did not settle on "multicultural" education until 1986. Earlier there was "cultural pluralism" and "intercultural education" to describe similar developments, in which the cultures of immigrant and minority groups were treated with some degree of respect. Many terms have thus arisen to encompass the reality that groups of different origin all form part of the American population, and in varying degrees part of a common culture and society. Multiculturalism is just the latest in this sequence of terms describing how American society, particularly American education, should respond to its diversity.

When we had to consider issues of race, ethnicity, and religion in American education prior to the 1950s, we did not, sad to say, have blacks much in mind. In the 1840s, 1850s, 1890s, and after the First World War in the days when the Ku Klux Klan boomed, the chief issues were whether Catholic children would attend public schools of a Protestant cast, whether children should be taught in German in public school, or whether private schools would have the right to exist. In the early 1900s in California, the question was whether to segregate Japanese children, and in the Depression a concern among Jews was their exclusion from elite colleges and medical schools. During all this time blacks either were educated in separate institutions, to which little attention was paid, or were a hardly noticeable presence in nonsegregated schools in the North and West; in either case they were virtually invisible to the majority.

But since the 1950s, when we speak of "diversity" in schooling, black students are at the heart of the matter. We have dealt in succession—though no serious issue is fully resolved, and none of these has been—with the dismantling of state-sponsored segregation, then with the overcoming of what we now call de facto segregation, then with attempts to improve educational achievement; and most recently we have grappled with the issues of curriculum raised by "multiculturalism" or its African American variant, "Afrocentrism." In the early phases of our public wrestling with the education of black students, curriculum was not a major concern: integration was the objective, and that did not necessarily imply any impact on curriculum. Later, achievement became the objective, and while that did affect curriculum, the impact was felt as much in science and mathematics as in social studies and English. In recent years, however, the curriculum, particularly in history, social studies, and humanities, has been at the heart of school conflicts around race.

Despite the importance of blacks in initiating a multiculturalist curriculum, multiculturalism has become much more than a black

cause. Joining in the attack on a received or traditional curriculum
(in truth not that old, but it doesn't take long for something to be
considered "traditional" in education) have been advocates of other
racial and ethnic groups and women. New waves of fashion in
literary studies and history find American school curricula in the
social studies and literature narrow, chauvinistic, dogmatic, and
devoid of respect and appreciation for the achievements of African
Americans and other minorities in the United States, of non-Euro-
peans in world history and literature, of women everywhere. It is
not only advocates of aggrieved groups who have launched an
attack on the curriculum of elementary and high schools. American
school achievement is sufficiently unimpressive that school critics
of all kinds call for curriculum reform. Yet despite all these participants in the campaign for multiculturalism, the movement is given
its force and vigor by our greatest domestic problem, the situation
of African Americans.

Multiculturalism is far from a neutral descriptive term, though it
is possible to describe the reality of minority and ethnic diversity
in this country neutrally. Multiculturalism covers a variety of ways
of responding to this reality, some so mild that they would probably
be acceptable to those who see themselves as the fiercest critics of
multiculturalism. But for most of those who advocate multiculturalism, it is a position-taking stance on the racial and ethnic diversity
of the United States. It is a position that rejects assimilation and the
"melting pot" image as an imposition of the dominant culture, and
instead prefers such metaphors as the "salad bowl" or the "glorious
mosaic," in which each ethnic and racial element in the population
maintains its distinctiveness. The maintenance of distinctiveness is
seen as a proper task of the school, rather than relegated to the
family or the ethnic school or neighborhood, as those who defend
assimilation would advocate.

Further along the multiculturalist spectrum from "acceptable" to
"upsetting," at least from the viewpoint of moderates, is the kind of

multiculturalism that emphasizes the oppression of the minority culture by the majority. Yet another development as one moves in the direction of a militant multiculturalism is the rejection of "additive multiculturalism" (adding a few great men or women from a minority group) in favor of "transformative multiculturalism," in which the entire history and culture of the United States is recast as dominantly shaped by race and ethnicity.[7] And then there are offshoots of multiculturalism, such as Afrocentrism, which also ranges from sensible proposals to include more about Africa in our school curricula to, at one extreme, what can only be called nonsense, such as insistence on African and Negro primacy in major technological achievements.

But no word can be constrained. Multiculturalism, for its advocates, becomes a new image of a better America, without prejudice and discrimination, in which no cultural theme linked to any racial or ethnic group has priority, and in which American culture is seen as the product of a complex intermingling of themes from every minority ethnic and racial group, and from indeed the whole world. To those who oppose multiculturalism's thrust, and in particular fear that it is fostering an education that emphasizes the faults and failures of America, multiculturalism has become a term describing all that has gone wrong in American education—indeed, more than that, in American public life generally. It has become an epithet denouncing those who do not appreciate what is good and decent about our society. And so we can find such a passage as, "Multiculturalists have succeeded not only in instituting stringent quotas in admissions offices and in faculty hiring, but in drastically changing the curriculum to eliminate what they call (in more polite moods) 'Eurocentric' bias."[8]

Obviously, the writer, Mark Gerson, who has become one of the chief chroniclers and celebrators of neoconservatism, does not consider himself a multiculturalist. But I assume even he believes that some attention to American minority groups in school curricula—

and more than we had in the 1950s—and some responsiveness to the changing racial and ethnic mix of students in schools are appropriate. So one gathers from his interesting account of a year he spent in an inner-city classroom.[9] Few, after all, believe otherwise. In this respect he too could be enrolled as a mild, if unwilling, multiculturalist. One can only reject the term if one insists no response whatsoever is necessary.

Gerson is able to so fully reject multiculturalism because he turns it into an all-embracing ideology encompassing every aspect of policy in regard to race, ethnicity, and gender that he opposes. In the process, he applies multiculturalism to matters that are not multiculturalism at all. Quotas and goals, whether in college admissions and hiring or in the economy generally, are not multiculturalism. Affirmative action has nothing to do with the recognition of cultures: it is part of a grand effort, the civil rights revolution, to provide justice to individuals and groups that have been deprived of equal treatment. It became in the minds of many who were supporters of this revolution a misguided effort. But conflating the two terms leads to intellectual confusion.

Affirmative action assumes nothing about culture—neither that it has been neglected nor that it should be recognized and celebrated. It is about jobs and admissions. The initial affirmative action requirements imposed by government on contractors—to advertise themselves as equal opportunity employers and to make a special effort to reach out to minorities in job recruiting—and the early voluntary efforts of colleges and universities to bring in more black students and faculty should both be seen as part of the effort to raise the economic condition of blacks, not as an effort to respond to their culture. There was no opposition among liberals to this earlier, milder form of affirmative action, and many of those now considered the strongest opponents of affirmative action accepted it, and still accept it. But as affirmative action rapidly grew into a matter of goals and timetables for employment and quotas for college admission, many supporters of affirmative action became its opponents. Their insistence that they still supported affirmative action, and were against only statistical goals and quotas, was dismissed in the public discourse. Affirmative action had become synonymous with goals and quotas, and the opponents of that development became simply opponents of affirmative action *tout court* in the mind of the public, and eventually in their own minds as well.

Words do change their meaning, and it became pointless to make the distinction between the two kinds of affirmative action, and even more pointless for those who still supported what to their minds was affirmative action to insist they were not opponents. Still, when one finds affirmative action encompassed in multiculturalism, one feels that the malleability of words has been taken to a useless extreme. The two developments are different in their origins. They are different in their objectives: justice for individuals and groups in one case, respect for the group in the other. They are different in the ways they were instituted: by government action in one case, by faculties and school boards and textbook publishers in the other.

It is not necessary to make "multiculturalism" cover every aspect of racial and ethnic and gender policy in the United States, and to turn it into a universal epithet denouncing every policy in regard to racial and ethnic groups one deplores. We have other perfectly good words, some predating "multiculturalism," such as the "balanced ticket," to describe the appointment of members of minority groups or of women to the slates of political parties; there is nothing new about the fact that politicians make appointments to show responsiveness to voting blocs.

Even though multiculturalism now has spread far beyond the schools, and far beyond its prime sense of respect for other cultures, for the purposes of this book I will confine it to this more restricted meaning. When I say multiculturalism has won, and that "we are all multiculturalists now," I mean that we all now accept a greater degree of attention to minorities and women and their role in American history and social studies and literature classes in schools. Those few who want to return American education to a period in which the various subcultures were ignored, and in which America was presented as the peak and end-product of civilization, cannot expect to make any progress in the schools.

Multiculturalism is, in its own way, a universalistic demand: All groups should be recognized. Some groups, however, have fallen below the horizon of attention, and other groups, defined by neither language nor ethnic or racial culture, have risen above it. So we find, for example, that multiculturalism is indifferent to the variety of ethnic groups of European origin but has come to encompass women and gays and lesbians. It is not easy to understand how this has happened.

Of course some limits had to be set on the multiculturalist demand for universal recognition and respect for group difference. There are, after all, thousands of cultures, if we associate a distinctive culture with every ethnic and racial group, and hundreds of them are present, to some degree, in the United States. The limit multiculturalism imposes on who will be recognized is set by the degree of prejudice and discrimination, or in stronger terms, "oppression," these groups have faced in the United States. Indeed, the opponents of multiculturalism label it "oppression studies." But even after one has confined the beneficiaries of multiculturalism to the oppressed, there is the problem of just who is oppressed, and there is still the tension with multiculturalism's universalistic claim that all groups must be recognized. At the University of California, Berkeley, when multiculturalists demanded that students should take a required course dealing with a number of major American ethnic and racial groups, the opponents of the required course riposted, "And what about Europeans?" The advocates of the requirement had to reluctantly concede. Europeans were added to the African Americans, Hispanics, Asian Americans, and Native Americans on the list of groups that could serve to fulfill the requirements of the course.

What was lost in that victory was any distinctions among the Europeans, some of whom had earlier been dominant, and some of whom had been subdominant. Indeed, one group of Europeans, Jews, were at one time considered the model of a minority group, and were so considered in all textbooks on American minorities. Italians, Greeks, Poles, and other Slavic groups could also have made a claim to victim status at one time or another, and certainly a claim to distinctiveness, whatever their degree of victimization. But in fact, few have made the claim in recent years. Except for Jews, who are also a religious group and have a long and important tradition of religious writings, no European group has been able to make much of a mark in ethnic and racial studies and programs. (Jews are dominantly but not exclusively European.) These groups had become American under the old regime of assimilation. To now demand recognition went against the grain of their experience, their expectations, their hopes for themselves in America. So they were all merged, for the purposes of ethnic studies at Berkeley, into the new category of Europeans.

If one explores the demands of multiculturalists, one discovers that, even among victims of oppression, not all groups are entitled to multicultural attention. Long before we became multiculturalists, the challenge to a monolithic and uniform American history celebrating its goodness and its triumphs came from those who emphasized not ethnic and racial division but class division. They explored the life of workers, their struggles, the bloody conflicts in which they were often engaged to improve their working conditions. This interest was undoubtedly stimulated by the Great Depression and the rise of new, powerful unions. The history of the working class and its organizations, such as the trade unions, became an important topic of interest to historians, and in time the volume of work on such matters among scholars began to filter down to the high schools and to affect modestly the history curriculum. So there were new sections in textbooks on the rise of the city, industrialism and manufacturing, mass immigration.

But the contrast between this revision of American history and the victory of multiculturalism is striking. Even though one hears the phrase "race, class, and gender" used to describe the new emphases being promoted in colleges—that was the rallying cry of those who fought the required Western Civilization course at Stanford University and replaced it with one giving more attention to race, class, and gender—class has certainly come in third, if it is evident at all, in the revision of curricula. The poor get into the new curriculum only if their poverty is associated with being female or nonwhite. Class as such plays little role in multiculturalism, an oddity that is worth some passing consideration. One suspects that the main reason is that "workers" are no longer seen as a deprived and oppressed and victimized group. It is rather the nonworking lower class that now takes the bottom victim position in the social ladder of class, and the worker and his institutions, such as trade unions, if not further specified by gender and race, are considered suspect and very likely prejudiced against minorities and women.

If it is not easy to understand how class came to be excluded from multiculturalism, similarly it is not easy to understand how women's studies came to be included. Women have been discriminated against in jobs and have been the victims of sexual harassment both on and off the job, but these civil rights issues are not part of multiculturalism if we take it to refer to culture. Women share, indeed shape, the culture of their families and their racial or ethnic group. To think of women as a uniformly deprived group because of their culture and regardless of their income, their race or ethnicity, their fathers, husbands, sons, requires something of a wrenching exercise in perspective. This exercise was not undertaken by earlier movements for the deprived and oppressed, such as socialist movements, or anticolonial movements.

Certainly one can speak of women's culture, as one can apply the term to almost any group, from a men's club and corporation to the entire West. There are some things that are held in common across vast stretches of population and area. Perhaps a distinctive women's language, a variant of the common tongue, is one. Multiculturalism in its origins—in Canada, for example—was thinking of language groups and cultural groups. When women's studies exploded, both women's studies and the new ethnic and racial studies could trace a common history, arising in the same decades, drawing on similar resentments, and a common new awareness of inequality. These similarities between racial and ethnic emphases in education and women's perspectives overweighed the enormous differences as categories between racial and ethnic groups on the one hand, and the entire female sex on the other.

Women's studies is part of multiculturalism, so large a part that it often outweighs all the rest. In the canon of received outrages perpetrated by multiculturalists—which has been put together by the opponents of multiculturalism to make their case—a hefty segment deals with offenses to the sensitivities of women. That women and racial and ethnic studies advocates are united is in one sense surprising. Women have fared much better in establishing large and respected fields in the humanities and social sciences, for example, than the racial and ethnic groups have. They have also done better in getting their viewpoint into elementary and high school texts. They have been more successful in getting academic jobs. (Asian American scholars also get a good number of jobs in a variety of fields, particularly in science and technology, but not because of their race or their expertise in Asian American studies.)

Things seep down from the elite colleges and universities to the high schools. In high school texts the role of women in American history now bulks larger than the role of African Americans, though it could be argued that African Americans, as a subject of American history and even as an organized and active and self-conscious element, have played a much greater role in American history than women, as an organized and self-conscious group. No matter. The place of women is firmly established and will not be reduced.[10]

One wonders whether the seepage down from the colleges and universities to the high schools and elementary schools will occur in the case of another group that has been embraced in multiculturalism, gays and lesbians. Gay and lesbian studies are beginning to make an impact, particularly in literary studies. Courses and programs are being established. Will we see the same effect on public education of this change in what is considered worthy of study and examination in higher education that we have seen in the case of women's studies? It is likely, though there will certainly be more conflict around the issue. The attempt in New York City to introduce gays and lesbians into a multicultural curriculum led to a fierce political battle and eventually to the resignation of the Chancellor of the New York City schools. But when one considers that the primary demand of multiculturalism is respect, and this respect is expected to strengthen tolerance and good relations among the individuals in the various groups whose character and achievements are to be displayed, one can see little reason why the process would stop short of gays and lesbians. If multiculturalism already extends beyond race and ethnic differences to include women's studies, why not the "cultures" of different "life-style" groups? It makes sense within the multicultural perspective. History moves toward ever greater equality, recognizing equality in ever new spheres, from the civil, to the political, to the economic, to the cultural. We have discovered and tried to make good the inequality in all these respects of the female sex. If progress is the spread of equality and liberty, one does not see how any good argument can be made against gay and lesbian claims. Behind the victory of multiculturalism, whatever the discomforts it brings, lie these two great principles, equality and liberty, and few want to be in the position of opposing their claims.

"Multiculturalism" is a term which many of us who have studied immigration and ethnic groups might have found perfectly satisfactory to cover our sense, some decades back, that American history and social studies should incorporate a larger recognition of American diversity. But terms take on a life of their own, totally unexpected by their original users. Multiculturalism has now become a contested term, an epithet to some, a banner to others. Multiculturalism of some kind there is, and there will be. The fight is over how much, what kind, for whom, at what ages, under what standards. To say one is "for" or "against" multiculturalism without going through all this effort is not to say much. The work of defining what kind, how much, for whom, and all the rest will continue to be done in national and state commissions, in state agencies, in local school boards, in individual schools by individual teachers, by textbook publishers and test makers. Having had some experience with a state commission reviewing a social studies curriculum, I have discovered how hard such work is, how various are our conceptions of America, how surprisingly we can disagree on what seem to me to be simple truths.

But overall I believe that short of the extremes there is a good deal of commonalty. The new America that multiculturalism, in its principal variants, envisages and is trying to establish as the America we learn about in schools will not, like the old, take it for granted that this is the best of all countries, as well as the strongest and the richest. We will become more self-conscious about making any claim to a distinctive virtue and superiority, and that is all for the best. There is much, after all, in the education of the old America that would grate on us today. The question that disturbs so many of us is whether the new multiculturalism will establish as a norm in education an all-embracing denunciation of the old

America, will spread a sense of resentment among many students, will lead to conflict greater than now exists between minorities and majorities. Will multiculturalism undermine what is still, on balance, a success in world history, a diverse society that continues to welcome further diversity, with a distinctive and common culture of some merit? I believe things will not come to that pass because the basic demand of the multiculturalists is for inclusion, not separation, and inclusion under the same rules—stretching back to the Constitution—that have permitted the steady broadening of what we understand as equality.

This book explores further, along the lines suggested in this chapter, the conflict over multiculturalism, delves deeper into the social situation from which it has emerged, and considers its implications for the future of American society. Chapter 2 tells the story of the conflict that erupted over new social studies guidelines in schools in New York State. In Chapter 3, I look in more detail at the four chief fears that properly concern us about multiculturalism in the curriculum. The subject of Chapter 4 is the recent conflict over the social studies curriculum in California, and the continuing efforts to establish national guidelines for curriculum, both of which demonstrate how hard it will be to resist the inexorable advance of some degree of multiculturalism. Chapter 5 explores some of the background to multiculturalism in older conflicts over the proper response to American diversity. In Chapter 6, I consider the past and future of assimilation as an ideal and reality, and argue that we never found a way to properly include African Americans in the great project that called for and fostered assimilation. In Chapter 7, I explore some of the consequences of this failure in the separation of blacks from whites and others in American society.

In Chapter 8, "We Are All Multiculturalists Now," I emphasize the inescapability of the phase we are now going through in American education and society in our centuries-old encounter with the questions of American racial and ethnic difference. It is not a phase we can embrace wholeheartedly, and I hope my own sense of regret that we have had to come to this will not escape the reader. The critics of multiculturalism have much wisdom on their side, and on many issues I join them. But we now pay for our failure to realize ideals, and the payment cannot be to insist ever more forcefully on the ideals, while ignoring the realities that contradict them. For a while we will be devoting great attention to American diversity in our education and public policy, not without some distortion and distention of the larger picture in the process. Despite this, I believe the elements of the American system that hold us together, in particular the basic political rules that we have adhered to for so long, will permit us to escape the extremes of rancor and divisiveness that the critics of multiculturalism fear.

2 ▲▲▲▲▲▲▲▲▲▲▲▲▲▲▲▲▲▲▲

THE NEW YORK STORY

The debate over multicultural education reached one of its peaks of stridency in New York State in the early 1990s, but it would be a mistake to consider the New York State situation unique. The battle over multiculturalism in education was as intense in California. There it focused on a group of social science textbooks for the elementary grades. They had been produced by Houghton Mifflin Company in response to a framework that had been developed by Charlotte Crabtree, a professor of education at the University of California, Los Angeles, and Diane Ravitch, a leading historian of education, educational reformer, and defender of the role of history in social studies education. Ravitch later served as an Assistant Secretary of Education in the Bush administration. The framework, which gave a much greater role to minorities and women than had previously been common in social studies curricular guidelines, had been approved at the state level in California without marked controversy. The textbooks, which followed the proposals of the new framework, were approved by the state, but it was up to the local school districts whether or not they should accept them, and it was at this level that the battle over content and multicultural acceptability became most intense.[1]

In New York State, matters never got that far. The battles there were over preliminary documents that were intended as guides to further steps in developing a new social studies curriculum. Despite the fact that the process began in 1989, it has still not been brought to completion. It stands to reason that the two most intense conflicts over multiculturalism in public education would take place in California and New York: New York was our largest state, with the largest immigrant population, until a few decades ago, when California replaced it in both respects. It also seems true that every issue of ethnic and racial group conflict becomes exaggerated in New York City, perhaps because the city is the center of the mass media and has developed a particularly acerbic style of ideological conflict.

The New York State controversy was exacerbated by a number of political errors and misjudgments by a new State Commissioner of Education, Thomas Sobol. His appointment had disappointed black and Hispanic state legislators, who had hoped the time had come for a black or Hispanic commissioner. To show his responsiveness to their concerns, Sobol appointed various committees to consider issues affecting these two minorities, among them a curriculum committee. This committee was composed of black and Hispanic educators and advocates, and it employed as a consultant one of the most militant Afrocentrists, Leonard Jeffries, Jr., a professor of black studies at the City College of the City University of New York, who was in time to become a focus of controversy in his own right.[2] The report of this committee, *A Curriculum of Inclusion,* denounced "Eurocentric" education in unmeasured language, breathed hostility toward what it considered European dominance, and called for a distinctive education for each racial and ethnic group (the "Europeans" being lumped as one), which would cover not only social studies but all fields of the curriculum. Its content and tone can be grasped from the first sentence of the Executive Summary: "African Americans, Asian Americans, Puerto Rican/ Latinos, and Native Americans have all been the victims of an intellectual and educational oppression that has characterized the culture and institutions of the United States and the European American world for centuries. Negative characterizations and the absence of positive references have a terribly damaging effect on the psyche of young people of African, Asian, Latino and Native American descent."[3] And so on.

The report was fiercely attacked. Leading the attack was Diane Ravitch. As an educational reformer, she advocated an emphasis on the narrative thrust of history rather than murky social studies concepts, and the highlighting of the more positive elements of American history: its democracy, constitutionalism, inclusiveness, tolerance. She had only recently completed her work on the California social studies curriculum, and this expressed the kind of emphases she felt were desirable in the teaching of American history. Ravitch, along with the distinguished historian Arthur Schlesinger, Jr., and joined by other leading American historians, issued a statement denouncing the report. They wrote: "The report, a polemical document, viewed division into racial groups as the basic analytical framework for an understanding of American history. It showed no understanding of the integrity of history as an intellectual discipline based on commonly accepted standards of evidence. It saw history rather as a form of social and psychological therapy whose function is to raise the self-esteem of children from minority groups." Most of the signers of the statement attacking *A Curriculum of Inclusion* were well-known liberals. The statement insisted that the signers were committed to "a pluralistic interpretation of American history and support for such shamefully neglected fields as the history of women, of immigration and of minorities." But, it asserted, "we are after all a nation—as Walt Whitman said, 'a teeming nation of nations.'" No one who calls for a nation-building curriculum can afford not to acknowledge American diversity, and this statement gave full acknowledgment to its significance for American history.[4]

A Curriculum of Inclusion was an easy target because of its intemperateness and its espousal of very doubtful claims of African primacy in various fields. It was attacked not only by historians but by the leading newspapers of New York City and the State. A second committee, more balanced, was then appointed. It was evenly divided between academics, some of whom had had little connection with social studies education at the elementary and high school levels, and teachers and administrators. It also included a leading critic of the first report, Arthur Schlesinger, Jr. (who served as a consultant to the committee, but participated in some of its meetings as an active and engaged member), and the historian Kenneth Jackson of Columbia University. Other members of the committee were Asa Hilliard III, a leading Afrocentrist who, however, played no role in its work, and Ali Mazrui, an African political scientist. I was also a member of this committee. While there is no necessary connection between ethnicity and attitudes on multiculturalism, it is revealing that about half of the committee were from groups not today considered minorities. The committee included three Hispanics, four African Americans, one Asian American, one Native American, and two Africans. The teacher and administrator contingent was two-thirds "non-Hispanic white," to use that odd census category ("Anglo" would scarcely serve to cover the Italian Americans, Jews, and so on who are now not considered minorities), and most were not, as far as one could tell from their biographical information and their activities on the committee, previously involved in any major way in furthering the multicultural thrust in the schools. Half the teachers and administrators were from districts like Gloversville, Liverpool, Cold Spring Harbor, Plattsburgh, and Dobbs Ferry, which did not have large minority enrollments. If I had been asked, I would also have signed the letter attacking the first report. So the committee, as far as one could tell, was not stacked in favor of the kind of multiculturalism demanded by the first committee.

It was clear that the function of the new committee was to repair the damage created by the first report, but it was also clear to all the participants that it was nevertheless expected to move in a more multicultural direction. Even if the membership of the committee was not stacked, one can scarcely imagine any mainstream committee, public or private, in the field of education today that would not take this tack.

Despite the wide range of points of view on the committee, its meetings and discussions were on the whole good-tempered. Few members espoused the more extreme positions that would outrage historians and be relatively easy to refute. The final report, as might be expected, was more moderate than that of the first committee, as reflected in its very title: *One Nation, Many Peoples: A Declaration of Cultural Interdependence.* It accepted the idea that this is one nation, and that it reflects an interdependence of cultures, but it also accepted the view that there are distinct cultures; it was not easy to reconcile these two orientations. Just how much "one nation" are we as against "many peoples"? Some members of the committee dissented from and attacked the report. The co-Chairmen of the committee, Edmund Gordon of Yale and Francis Roberts, Superintendent of Schools, Cold Spring Harbor, proposed, in order to avoid dissents, that the report need not be "accepted" or "rejected," simply issued, with whatever additional statements members wished to append, but Schlesinger's and Jackson's comments amounted to full-fledged dissents.[5]

The new report did not escape denunciation almost as fierce as that which greeted the first. Battle lines had already been set by the first report, positions had been chosen, making it impossible for the second committee to produce a document that would gain acceptance among the critics of the first. Consider the political context:

The committee had to moderate the extreme positions of the first document. But to withdraw too far would lead to denunciation by black and Hispanic advocates, and, after all, the entire enterprise had been launched to respond to their complaints and concerns.

Additional factors played a role in the kind of report that was finally issued. Half its members, and more than half of those regularly present, were school teachers and administrators, and all of them more or less accepted the legitimacy, the acceptability, indeed the necessity of multiculturalism. The curriculum they taught, and which we reviewed, was to an outsider (such as myself) already sufficiently multicultural. Working in schools and in the context of current educational discussion and practice, they accepted without dispute that multiculturalism was the way to go in education, and many of their educational practices already embodied it. It was, oddly, only among the academics, who had little or no role in public school education, that substantial debate ensued over the substance of multiculturalism. Those members of the committee who worked in schools seemed less concerned about the degree of multicultural tilt in the report than about what it meant for the practical work of teachers and administrators. New curricular guidelines would mean that schoolteachers, who had been teaching a curriculum that itself had just recently been adopted after a long process of consultation, would now have to learn a new one, and prepare their students for new tests. The issue of just what was in the curriculum, or in the tests, seemed to concern them less than the fact that the curriculum and the tests would be new, and would therefore pose a threat to teachers.

Pondering what I might write in my own statement attached to the report, I wondered why we had heard so little from schoolteachers and administrators about multiculturalism itself and its legitimacy, an issue that was already receiving widespread attention in the mass media. For some guidance, I called a member of the committee, a supervisor of social studies education in New

York City, whose participation in the committee suggested no particular commitment to multiculturalism, and asked why we had not heard more from the schoolteachers and administrators in our discussions. He responded in effect that he didn't care that much *what* his students read, as long as they could read and write. The response was sobering, and put before me the stark realities under which our teachers and administrators work in New York City. He himself works in one of the poorest districts of the city, but those members of the committee from suburban and upstate schools were equally accepting of the multicultural thrust.

Did the new report warrant the widespread denunciation that greeted it? Its quality, all could agree, was not distinguished. But there was no smoking gun, nothing like the inflammatory opening words of *A Curriculum of Inclusion.* Our report wended its way in educationese through various uncontroversial themes, as is typical of all educational curricular reports, and avoided inflammatory language. But the main thrust of the report, in its effort to move away from, but not too far from, the first report, was to emphasize "multiple perspectives" in the teaching of history. That would not arouse historians particularly: they are used to multiple perspectives. But these multiple perspectives were to be taught to elementary and high school students, and they were to be ethnic and racial: the perspectives of Native Americans, of African Americans, of Mexican Americans, Asian Americans, others. Multiple perspectives, apparently, no longer seemed to include the point of view of workers as against employers, or urbanites as opposed to suburbanites, or small-towners versus farmers, or Northeasterners as contrasted with Southerners. These perspectives and others of course could also have been incorporated into the "multiple perspectives." How a common history would emerge from these various perspectives, which were now to be critically examined by schoolchildren under the guidance of teachers who, we had been warned, would be dismayed at the thought of having to revise their

▲ ▲ ▲

teaching to accommodate new guidelines and who would find the requirement to present multiple perspectives a challenge, was not clear.

The report did point to common elements in American history and society, but rather weakly: "The social studies will very likely continue to serve nation-building purposes, among others, even as we encourage global perspectives. With efforts to respect and honor the diverse and pluralistic elements in our nation, special attention will have to be given to those values, characteristics, and traditions we share in common. Commitment to the presentation of multiple perspectives in the social studies curriculum encourages attention to the traditional and dominant elements in our society, even as we introduce and examine minority elements which have been neglected." And: "The program should be committed to the honoring and continuing examination of democratic values as an essential basis for social organization and nation-building." When the report speaks of the Constitution and the Bill of Rights, it emphasizes the struggle to achieve and realize rights, rather than celebrating these founding charters as guaranteeing them. That would have been found objectionable by some members of the committee. The report's emphasis (or overemphasis) on difference was also somewhat muted: "In recent decades many in the United States from European and non-European backgrounds have been encouraging a more tolerant, inclusive, and realistic vision of American identity than any that has existed in the past. This identity, committed to the democratic principles of the nation and nation-building in which all Americans are engaged, is progressively evolving toward . . . a new model marked by respect for pluralism and awareness of the virtues of diversity."

Commissioner Sobol, building on such elements in the report (and on the dissents, which he quoted approvingly), was able to make follow-up proposals to the Board of Regents of the State of New York that no critic of the excesses of multiculturalism would have found objectionable, and most would approve. These next steps, he asserted emphatically, "do not recommend . . . trashing the centrality of the West, an Afrocentric curriculum, ethnic cheerleading and separatism, distorting history, a study of American history based on ethnicity and culture alone." This was stretching the report somewhat, and might have discommoded some of the members of the committee, but it did not require any repudiation of the report.

But none of these mollifying elements helped. The report and the entire multicultural enterprise were attacked in a cover story in *Time* magazine, in a long editorial in *The New Republic,* and in newspapers and television news programs throughout the state.[6] Governor Mario Cuomo also attacked it. On the whole, the reception was hostile. One of the problems the press has in dealing with such reports is that it doesn't read them. Press reporting tends to consist of who said what about the report, who attacked and who defended it. This report, because of its relative blandness, had few items the press could seize on. But in its efforts to indicate how language in syllabi or texts could be more sensitive, the report was unwise enough to suggest that the term "enslaved persons" could replace "slaves" and that Thanksgiving should be seen from the point of view of the Indians as well as the pilgrims. This was not much, but these were easy objects for attack and ridicule. In general, the entire stance of press and media treatment is to emphasize difference rather than commonalties, conflict rather than areas of agreement, to polarize issues even more than they already are by selecting or publicizing extreme statements. Multiculturalism is no exception to this pattern: Afrocentrism has many variants and could mean many things, but from the point of view of press treatment it means only outlandish nonsense (of which there is unfortunately a good deal in Afrocentrism).

The aftermath of this report was yet other committees and other reports, and the curricular guides that our committee reviewed in

1991 — and that seemed already sufficiently multicultural to me — are apparently still the ones that guide social studies teaching in New York State. But there is no question that whatever the denunciations that greeted this report, multiculturalism was the way that education was going in the public schools, in social studies and language studies. Indeed, part of the media response to *One Nation, Many Peoples* was to send reporters to the schools to find out just what was going on. The discovery was that while the report was proposing multiculturalism, it was already fully ensconced in "majority-minority" schools — those with majorities of minority students — and hardly less prominent in others.[7] And could one have been surprised, when city schools are overwhelmingly minority, when the head of almost every big-city school system is black or Hispanic, when many teachers, as one finds from casual discussion, find that material on blacks and other minorities engages their students' interests more fully than the more traditional curriculum materials?

The incoming president of the New York City Board of Education, Carl McCall, who was no militant, was reported as saying, "I think an Afrocentric curriculum, which pays attention to and exposes other groups and other heritages, can be positive." Mr. McCall "compared such schools to afternoon Hebrew classes that his Jewish classmates attended in the Roxbury section of Boston, where he grew up. The Hebrew classes, he said, fostered a cultural identity. Although they were not public, he said, they could serve as models for neighborhoods that 'don't have the resources' to set up private schools."

"Mr. McCall strongly endorsed a state panel's recent report [our report] calling for a social studies curriculum that would pay greater attention to nonwhite cultures. He still keeps his dog-eared high school history book that explains its omission of African and American Indian cultures by saying that they were 'less advanced and their influence less notable than the cultures we've studied.'"[8]

One could add other testimonials, from members of other big-city school boards, and from superintendents of big-city schools. Many of those who were then denouncing the report simply seemed unaware of how far advanced the big-city schools were on the road to multiculturalism. Every day's newspapers brought more news. The SATs, one student reported, now concentrate on the "achievements of minorities, women, and third-world countries, bemoan the shortcomings of American society, and advance fashionable causes." The questions require knowledge of Zora Neale Hurston, Ralph Ellison, Richard Wright, Gwendolyn Brooks, Lorraine Hansberry, and Jackie Robinson (he comes up twice). The fiction reading is from Maya Angelou.[9] Of course schools that expect their students to do well on SATs will have to adjust their curriculum accordingly.

A few years before our report, Diane Ravitch and Chester Finn, Jr., had published an interesting book, *What Do Our Seventeen-Year-Olds Know?* which simply determined, through a national survey in 1986, just what facts about history American students knew at that time and listed them in order by the percentage of students in the survey who knew these facts. More students could identify Harriet Tubman than could identify Winston Churchill or Stalin, more knew she had run the underground railway than knew that George Washington commanded the American army in the Revolution, or that Lincoln wrote the Emancipation Proclamation. In 1993 a *U.S. News and World Report* survey found that while 90 percent of American undergraduates could identify Rosa Parks, only 25 percent knew the author of the phrase "government of the people, by the people, for the people" and only 18 percent could identify as much as a single justice of the Supreme Court.[10]

A report at the time on a conference on cultural pluralism at Wheelock College in Boston brought the news that the participants, asked to list the "five American authors they believed most necessary for a quality education," put Toni Morrison in second place, Maya Angelou in third. Mark Twain was still in first place. The rest of the top ten line-up were Alice Walker, John Steinbeck, Malcolm X, Richard Wright, James Baldwin, Langston Hughes, and William Faulkner. At the conference, the then-President of Wesleyan University, William M. Chace, said of multiculturalism: "As an issue, we know it's on the way to triumph."[11]

The mass of materials that flowed in on us as we worked on our report gave evidence of how well established multiculturalism already was in New York State. One of the documents we were given listed teachers' guides available from the State Education Department, in addition to the social studies syllabi. Of the seven publications available, four dealt with minorities and women. The most substantial was a three-volume publication on the teaching of the Holocaust. A survey of in-service workshops taken by teachers in 1990–91 showed American history and European history workshops had been taken by 156 participants, while workshops on African history, black studies, ethnic studies, multicultural education, and cultural diversity had been taken by 264.

That was the reality, and remains the reality. What impressed me was the strength of multiculturalism, the apparent inevitability of multiculturalism. This had to moderate one's response: Simple denunciation, it seemed, would no longer do, though there was plenty more of that to come in the following years.

We remain in the midst of the controversy over multiculturalism, and it is not easy to discern the significance of this development and where it might lead. Nevertheless, to try to make some sense of the situation is essential: It is one of the shaping forces in American education today.

3 ▲▲▲▲▲▲▲▲▲▲▲▲▲▲▲▲

WHAT IS AT STAKE IN
MULTICULTURALISM?

Almost everyone today agrees that as against a curriculum whose only objective is Americanization and assimilation we need something else, something which is more inclusive. In an essay a few years ago, the philosopher Charles Taylor — particularly sensitized to this issue because he teaches at English-speaking McGill, in French-speaking Quebec, in largely English-speaking Canada — described multiculturalism as an expression of a "politics of recognition."[1] Groups, racial and ethnic, and women want to see themselves in the curriculum, in those who write it, in those who teach it. Few attack this new thrust head-on. But what will this new emphasis on multiculturalism, on "recognition," do to our efforts to teach our children truth and the best way to reach it, to promote American unity, to encourage civic harmony? And how will it affect the ability of minority students to learn and achieve? These are the four big questions about multiculturalism, and they reveal its critics' fears: That an emphasis on multiculturalism will teach our children untruths, that it will threaten national unity, that it will undermine civic harmony (to the extent we have it), and that it will do nothing to raise the achievement of the groups expected to benefit from it.

34

It is easy enough to reject extreme positions, whether Afrocentric or Eurocentric. Clearly we should not base the social studies curriculum in the elementary and high schools on pure fantasies about the role of Africa and blacks in world history, something equivalent perhaps to the Book of Mormon or the myths of the black Muslims as elaborated by Elijah Muhammed. Yet in some schools this is already occurring. A few years ago a black student at Harvard came to see me to ask what could be done about the fact that Harvard students do not know that blacks discovered (or I suppose one should say "encountered") the New World long before Columbus. I could only say I thought this supposed truth about early African sea voyages was highly unlikely, as unlikely as that St. Brendan got here before Columbus, and that it probably plays the same role for some blacks as St. Brendan's mythical trip to the New World plays for some Irishmen. I do not think I had much influence on her.

In any case, it is probably more important that students—at Harvard and elsewhere—learn how we properly come to conclusions than that they are fed the "correct" conclusion. But desirable as such an approach would be, I don't think elementary and high school teachers for the most part can properly instruct their students in these matters. Further, I suspect it is more difficult to engage student interest on questions of inference from evidence— on the complicated issues of how we test fossils for age, for example, or how we assess the authenticity of documents—than on the story itself. The best possible accounts should be set before students. But in an age when authority is disputed in so many areas, it is likely that Afrocentric exaggeration will play a substantial role in inner-city schools, and we will continue to see myths taken as truths.[2]

At the other extreme, I would reject a curriculum that gives the same place to European history that it held in the 1940s. Many details in that history have become insignificant or irrelevant for today's students. I assume there are still some people who find the history and social studies of the 1940s, '50s, and '60s adequate to our current circumstances and needs, and who regret that high schools today do not give as much attention to European history as they did in the late 1930s, when I took a required course in the subject at James Monroe High School in the Bronx. Indeed, there is no European History as a required course any more in the New York State high schools—it was replaced first by World History and then by Global Studies. And so our high school students today will know almost nothing about the rise of the dynastic and absolute state in Europe, the war of the Spanish succession, the rise of Prussia and Russia, the unification of Italy and Germany, and a variety of other topics. I regret this because I like history, even when—indeed particularly when—it is remote. But I can make no argument on principled educational grounds that these and other topics should be restored. Just as I could have made no argument on principled educational grounds, despite my love for such antiquarian materials as the War of the Roses, that the history of England, which used to be taught as a required course in New England high schools at the turn of the century, should not be replaced by a broader course in European History, as it was.

There is an important difference, however, between the two positions I reject. The multicultural or Afrocentric extreme is based in too large part on fantasy, whereas the Eurocentric extreme is based not on fantasy but on a commitment to subjects of study that have lost significance and meaning for our lives today, and in particular for many of our students' lives. Nevertheless, a good part of the Eurocentric curriculum that the critics of multiculturalism want to hold on to is indeed crucially relevant to our world today. Our world has been shaped, and is being shaped, by science and technology in the world of production, by distinctive instruments of finance in the world of the economy, by the power of the ideals of constitutionalism, democracy, and human rights in the world of politics. All of this first established itself in Europe and, owing to the European expansion between the fifteenth and twentieth centuries, spread throughout the world.

Origins do not make a prima facie case for inclusion in a curriculum. Afrocentrists make much of the fact that the earliest ancestors of humans first emerged in Africa, according to our current research. (Earlier, it was thought to be Java, or China, where the first of these humanlike ancestors emerged, and other parts of the world may come forward as candidates as paleontologists explore further.) But where our species first emerged seems to have little bearing on subsequent human history. Similarly, if some kind of ur-language, according to some current theories, first emerged in Africa, that too has little bearing on the subsequent history of language and literature. Whatever the achievements of ancient Egypt, and they are great and awesome indeed, they have little connection with our world today, or the world of the last thousand years, and very little even to do with current-day Egypt, except perhaps to provide tourist revenue. And whatever the scale of these ancient Egyptian achievements, it is doubtful that persons of the black race played any great role in them.

The European origins listed above, on the other hand, are close to us chronologically, and there is much today we cannot understand—for example, the political problems of the Third World—without understanding European history. Attitudes toward this primacy of Europe may differ, but one cannot dispute that European ideas, power, and expansion account for the fact that almost all modern states share similar ideals and similar approaches to the realization of their ideals. So an emphasis on the primacy of Europe has a very different character from an emphasis on the primacy of Africa in defining and shaping our world.

But then, after the exercise of rejecting the extremes, what are we to do about social studies education in the schools? Where along the road from Eurocentrism to Afrocentrism do we pitch our tent? My approach to this question is to raise a series of subordinate questions, all of which are important in trying to define our stance on multiculturalism.

Is truth the only test for a social studies curriculum? "Teach the truth" would be an easy answer to our problem, and it is one which in principle both the extreme multiculturalists and their critics would accept. Both lay claim to the truth. The more vociferous proponents of multiculturalism claim that they do not challenge the truth; they rather seek to establish a truth which has been ignored, hidden, the more extreme say "stolen." They believe that the injustice of racial discrimination is being perpetuated in the curriculum, and that many achievements attributed to Egyptians, Greeks, or others were in truth accomplished by blacks.

The critics of multiculturalism also rest their case on truth, and see in multiculturalism a fatal disregard for the mechanisms by which agreement as to the nature of reality is reached — call it "the scientific method." In the insistence by multiculturalists, such as the authors of *A Curriculum of Inclusion,* that the role of the West, Western thought, Western philosophy, Western achievements have been exaggerated, and that this exaggeration has damaged students whose origins are not in European countries, critics see a challenge to rationality and science, the chief heritage of the West. The proponents of multiculturalism, on the other hand, argue that diversity of viewpoint on the nature of "truth" is the greatest strength of America, and that further recognition of this diversity, and its ever greater reach, will not harm polity, culture, or economy. Quite the contrary, they claim America will be strengthened by it.

Truth is a more difficult ground for the social studies today than it once was. In academic field after field, truths are constantly challenged, because they are based on doubtful assumptions, or use flawed methodologies, or reflect hidden prejudices. Mathematics and the sciences are comparatively immune from this assault, though some critics of science, including historians and philosophers of science, have argued that even the truths of science are not as objective as is commonly accepted and are not beyond the power and influence of ordinary human interests and passions. Even these critics of science, I would guess, take it on faith that the bridge over which they are driving will not collapse, and that a good cardiologist should be consulted when one develops a heart problem.

But in other fields, the assault on established doctrines, procedures, and findings is serious. Few go to the extreme of saying that truth is simply what we prefer because of our own interests and what we impose because of our power (though perhaps some deconstructionists go that far). It is clear that scholarly and scientific authority does not carry the weight it once did among nonexperts. The fact that most of the people working in an established discipline, using its accepted procedures and approaches, have come to certain conclusions no longer determines the truths we accept.

Furthermore, no one really insists that truth is the only criterion for judgment on curriculum in the social studies. We have, after all, other key objectives: objectives related to citizenship, the creation of national unity, the discouragement of group antagonism. If "truth" undermines these objectives—for example, by concentrating on the fact that the rich have more influence on public authorities than the poor, or that one group has discriminated, and continues to discriminate, against another, or that this kind of treatment could well justify hatred of one group for another, or disrespect for public authority—then what?

Truth is an uncertain and incomplete guide. Bear in mind that we are speaking here of the education of children and adolescents, age groups which, in the past, have been told stories that were not quite so, but they were nevertheless told the stories either for their own good or for the good of society. We used to tell the story of George Washington and the cherry tree, as a way of teaching respect for honesty and for the father of our country. It has been known to be a myth for a long time. We are now told we should tell other stories, with other moral lessons.

In the New York State syllabus there is a reference to the influence of the Iroquois or Hodenosaunee federation on the framers of the Constitution. I believe—on the basis, I will confess, of what authorities I have read have said (or rather, on the basis of reading those who quote authority) and because it just seems doubtful to me on the basis of a very general knowledge of history—that the influence of Native Americans on our Constitutional framework was insignificant, perhaps nonexistent. I would think that, because of their education, the framers were more influenced by their knowledge of federations in classic Greek history. But how important is it that students should know that? If students believe that knowledge of the Hodenosaunee federation influenced some framers, and if this belief raised Native Americans in the esteem of their fellow students, would that be a justification for teaching the story? Might one accept the story for young elementary school students, to whom we teach so much about Native Americans, but not for students in junior high or high school?

A few years ago a controversy arose over the movie *The Liberators,* which depicted black soldiers as being among those who liberated the concentration camps. The movie was promoted as a way to improve black–Jewish relations. What should we have done about the assertions of historians who know the details that the facts were not exactly as presented, that black soldiers were not among those who first reached the camps? In a larger sense, black soldiers were in the army that liberated the camps. Should the movie have been shown to children? I am not taking a stand on the matter, but one must respect the good will of those who made the movie.

All of these questions about age-appropriateness and helpful civics lessons do not address a far more serious problem: That on the largest themes in the American past, such as the weight to be given to class, property, wealth, and race in shaping the Constitution, and the conflicts that have divided the nation in the two hundred years since, there will always be disagreement, and sometimes quite basic disagreement; even well-informed adults find it hard to agree on what is the simple and unvarnished "truth."

Difficult as it is to implement them at the lower grades, and indeed in high school, we cannot escape "multiple perspectives." Students will raise them, even if the teachers and textbooks don't. One cannot have any great confidence that many teachers will be able to deal with these multiple perspectives with skill and balance, and one would not want the multiple perspectives to replace the simple facts. There are simple facts—dates, names, places, numbers—that students should know, and it is tempting to envisage an education in which we stick to them, rather than expand into interpretations and perspectives and overall evaluations. That temptation is particularly understandable when we contemplate the struggle over national standards in history (see Chapter 4). But none of us would be satisfied with a history that is only a catalog of the facts. And even then we would have to consider and argue over what facts, what names, what events to include, and how even the catalog would affect a student's understanding of the nation.

There are other objectives in teaching that affect our commitment to the simple truth. And so we come to a second question:

What weight do we give to national unity in the formation of a public school curriculum? A great fear among critics of multiculturalism is that its overemphasis will undermine the success of assimilation, which in the past has united immigrants of diverse cultures into Americans with a common culture and common loyalty. Many of these critics come out of a school system, as I do myself, in which there was simply no acknowledgment of anything besides the common culture and the common loyalty. There was a school pageant, often referred to in studies of Americanization, in a Dearborn school in which diverse immigrants, each dressed in a distinctive costume, entered a huge melting pot on the school stage and emerged on the other side all dressed alike.[3] That was certainly the ambition of Americanization in the 1920s and '30s. Not only was the history and culture of immigrants ignored but their practices were commonly regarded as inferior, and derided by teachers. It didn't matter that one came from a home in which one had coffee and a roll for breakfast; one should have orange juice and milk. There was no bilingualism in schools, at best only the "steamer class" (an English immersion class; the "steamer" referred to the ships in which the immigrants had come) to prepare students for rapid entry into regular classrooms.

When we speak of the importance of national unity, I think at the extreme what we fear is disloyalty in war. In the days of assimilation and Americanization perhaps we exaggerated how much national unity was necessary to fight foreign wars effectively. The kind of hysteria that drove the German language from the schools and German words from our speech in World War I did not recur in World War II. We had no doubt of the loyalty of German Americans and Italian Americans in that war, even when we were fighting against their homelands. Our attitudes toward Japanese Americans were, sadly, quite a different matter; they were treated far more severely than German Americans had been in World War I.

Did our acceptance of American ethnic groups whose homelands were our enemies in Europe hurt our war effort? And how much national unity does the United States need at the end of the twentieth century anyway? We have become looser about the matter, with the end of the Cold War. Perhaps we don't expect to fight any more world wars. Even if our relations with Japan worsen, we are more willing to accept without attributions of disloyalty the fact that Japanese Americans may look upon Japan's economic success more kindly than other Americans do.

Further, how confident are we that a curriculum which ignores or downplays differences produces a stronger national loyalty than one which pays attention to differences? During World War I, it was thought that the way to achieve national unity was to attack fiercely any ties of Americans to their European culture; but in World War II, in the face of Hitler's oppression of so many European ethnic groups, the ties of many Americans to their European homelands was used to *strengthen* the war effort.

I do not think multiculturalism is doing much to affect, one way or another, the attitudes of European-origin ethnic groups to the United States. It is possible that an excessive dose of multiculturalism is leading to disaffection among these groups and encouraging some antiestablishment extremists in their belief that malign secret powers are manipulating the school system, trying to get into the heads of their children to brainwash them into thinking this country owes something to minorities. In this respect multiculturalism may be increasing disunity. This is not unlikely, but I have seen no evidence of such effects.

Asian Americans are also not likely to be affected by multiculturalism. Chinese students (and others) will be told of the exploitation of Chinese workers in the building of the transcontinental railway; Japanese students will learn about the shameful episode of the relocations camps, which appears in every American history textbook. One doubts that these new emphases will affect Chinese and Japanese students much.

African Americans, Hispanic Americans, and women are the chief groups whose profile is raised by multiculturalism. When we consider potential threats to national unity because of minority group disaffection and possible disloyalty, we would have to think first of African Americans, Puerto Ricans, and Mexicans. But do we have any good grounds to fear that greater attention to their history and mistreatment will weaken their attachment to the United States? One knows that blacks and Hispanics are disproportionately to be found in the American armed forces, which also work more energetically and effectively than any other institution in American society to offer them avenues for advancement. One can think of many factors that might lead to resentment and disaffection among African Americans and Puerto Ricans and Mexican Americans. We nevertheless want a balanced treatment of the history of these groups in the United States. We have to tell the story of slavery, discrimination, and prejudice, and how the United States annexed half of Mexico, and Puerto Rico. But in any scale of serious disaffection and disloyalty among minority ethnic groups — let us say, a scale ranging from the Romansch in Switzerland to the Chechens in Russia — I believe one would have to rate the propensity of our major minorities to disloyalty pretty far down, well below the Chechen level.

Many influences reach students quite independent of the public school, and the majority of them today insist on and celebrate difference. Multiculturalism has become a generalized marketing tool. Conceivably the public school could serve as a counterforce to these influences from mass media, sports, politics, and other spheres, but how much do we know about the relative effectiveness of the public school in shaping a common identity, a common loyalty? Was it more effective when it tried harder to do so? Perhaps during World War I, George M. Cohan songs and the like did more to create the common American culture than Americanization programs in schools; we don't know. I am reminded of the fact that parochial schools were once thought by many to promote disloyalty, or an alternative loyalty. We now think that the best patriots (even chauvinists) may come from parochial schools.

The relation between our direct efforts to create loyalty and unity through school curricula and the making of patriots is not simple. There is, it seems, no necessary contradiction between an education that promotes a distinctive loyalty, different from national loyalty, as in the case of the parochial school, and a commitment to the interests of the nation and a willingness to participate in its defense or its military ventures in the name of defense. Of course it depends on the character of the distinctive education a group gets. One can imagine—in fact I am sure there are examples of it—a kind of multicultural education which, if it took hold, would make students unwilling to serve in a national army, or indeed a local police force. But it is not only the formal education that might lead to such a result. There is also the education given by the media, by rap groups, by one's own experience with the government or the police.

I do not dismiss fears that a necessary degree of national cohesiveness would be threatened as a result of some kinds of multicultural education. But some of the dominant trends in multicultural education—for example those that emphasize the contributions of various ethnic groups—should not have this effect, and might well strengthen national loyalty. If the emphasis moves to oppression, discrimination, grievance, certainly the effects could well undermine national unity. One would have to see more examples of multicultural curricula, more examples of how they operate concretely in the schools, before one could make a judgment.

National disunity is a reasonable fear, but perhaps an exaggerated one. But even in the absence of a national enemy, there may be a degree of divisiveness that can be dangerous. So we come to the third question:

Does multiculturalism undermine civic harmony? The issue here is not disloyalty in the face of a war against Germany or Japan, such as we fought in the 1940s, but the interracial and intergroup distrust and conflict that we see all around us. Some critics of multiculturalism fear that its emphasis will lead to greater internal divisiveness, to the Quebec syndrome, or the Yugoslav syndrome. We have a history of thirty years of race riots, in which blacks or other minorities rise up against some outrage, real or rumored. Does multicultural education promote the attitudes that make this more likely? Again, so much depends on the details, just what is in the curriculum, just how the teacher uses it. There is no question that the emphasis on oppression, discrimination, prejudice, grievance would have this result. And yet the existence of discrimination and prejudice is also reality—truth, if you will.

Teachers will disagree on how much weight to put on this reality, in the past and today, as will parents and minority leaders. As a member of the New York State curriculum committee, I argued that the mistreatment of African Americans, Mexican Americans, and others was certainly part of American history and could not be ignored, but that if one looked at the larger picture of the history of the United States, one saw greater and greater inclusion, less and less discrimination, a steady increase in the protection of the rights of minorities, and constitutional protections and guarantees becoming more and more effective. That was the truth, as I saw it, and that was the point to be emphasized in the curriculum.

But a reputable scholar on the committee, an anthropologist of Mexican parentage, argued the opposite. He did not give the same weight to the improvement or the changes that had occurred as I did. I assume he could recognize some of the specifics that supported my argument—that our immigration laws had abandoned racial restrictions, or that the civil rights movement had established nondiscrimination as the law of the land—but how firm, he asked, were these changes, how accepted? He could have pointed to the fact that Haitians were not treated in immigration matters as well as Cubans, that blacks were still treated differently according to current tests of discrimination in their efforts to get jobs or buy houses, and so on. I pointed to the protections of the Constitution; he expressed fears that a white backlash would limit or overthrow these protections. Our committee ended up with the weak compromise that we should teach "multiple perspectives." Of course there are multiple perspectives in the social sciences, but is that good enough for elementary and high school students? Aren't some perspectives much better supported than others? So I think— which brings us back to the argument for truth, and all the problems connected with that.

I would like to add to the claims that truth makes on the curriculum the claims of civic harmony. What would be better for young blacks to believe: That everyone is against them? That all their protections are shams? That whites will always stop them from getting ahead? That their oppression has been scarcely reduced since the days before the civil rights revolution and the Civil Rights Act? Or would it be better for them to believe the reverse: That the vast majority of Americans wish them well? That their civil rights are protected by the laws of the land? That their historic oppression at the hands of citizens and law enforcement officials is slowly but steadily declining?

There is a question of practical utility here. For their own good, their own progress, I believe that it would be better for young blacks to believe that there has been improvement in their situation, that their opportunities are greater than before, rather than the reverse. This is aside from the fact that the evidence I believe overwhelmingly supports this conclusion. It would be better for them to believe that the Ku Klux Klan and other antiblack groups are minuscule sects rather than the wave of the future in which their rights will be swept away.

Unfortunately, some apocalyptic and paranoid beliefs are widespread. A substantial minority of the black population, according to public opinion surveys, believes that AIDS is a white plot against blacks.[4] Spike Lee and Sister Souljah, who are among the most prominent and effective teachers of young blacks today, seem to believe this, or at least are willing to credit the story. So even if we thought it both true and better for minorities to believe in the ever greater inclusiveness of American society, forces outside the public school tell a different story.

I know what is better for all of us to believe, from the standpoint of civic harmony. But others think that civic harmony should not be given primacy as an ideal: they believe in the slogan so prominently displayed in the disorders that broke out after the policemen who beat Rodney King were found innocent, "No justice, no peace." How will we convince those displaying this slogan that a substantial measure of justice already exists, and that the sphere of justice is constantly expanding? How do we get that point of view into a multicultural curriculum?

Consider the question of whether blacks are discriminated against in the imposition of the death penalty. Reputable civil rights groups believe this and have tried to make use of this supposed fact in appealing death sentences. I think the evidence shows otherwise.[5] But what answer is there to resolving such a question other than arguing the point in the forums that are available for curriculum formation and review? We will, I believe, continue to wage a steady battle over curricular details, between those who believe that harmful untruths have worked their way into the curriculum and should be removed, and others who believe that a suppressed truth is finally being recognized. I see no alternative course of resolution.

After truth, unity, harmony—objectives that we hope will be advanced by education—we come to an objective of education that both multiculturalists and their critics agree is crucial, and for which the evidence of education's influence is quite strong: Making a good living. We all believe that earnings depend on getting an education, or at least on sustained attendance in educational institutions, and this conclusion is as well supported in the social sci-

▲ ▲ ▲

ences as any we have. Advocates of multiculturalism claim that the ineffectiveness of education for many minority children, and their poor attendance in school, could be overcome if minority children saw themselves in the curriculum. Thus we come to the fourth question:

Do students have to see themselves in the curriculum if they are to learn effectively? The argument here is that when students do not see members of their own group in textbooks and among their teachers and administrators, school becomes foreign and distant to them, and perhaps is seen as hostile. A related question is, must students have high self-esteem in order to learn? And is this self-esteem enhanced by learning about the achievements of members of their own group in school, regardless of how insignificant those achievements are?

I think these questions require us to explore a preliminary question: What do we mean by the "self"? The assumption of the multiculturalist enthusiasts is that the self refers to the racial and ethnic self. But of course we are all made up of many selves. There is the self that prefers tennis to baseball, the self that prefers rock to classical music, the self that prefers science to social studies, that is poor rather than well-to-do, suburban rather than inner-city, Southern rather than Northern, Lutheran rather than Baptist, and so on and so on. There are multiple selves, not all of which can be represented in the teachers and the curriculum. The assumption in multiculturalism is that of these many selves, one is dominant. Consequently, it is not necessary to represent the musical, athletic, regional, class, or religious self, because the racial or ethnic self is central and decisive. If the racial or ethnic self is not represented in the curriculum, education cannot occur, or cannot occur effectively.

There are answers to this argument, answers I have given myself. But I am afraid they are debaters' answers, and will not reach the core of this issue. Thus, one could say that not everyone can be presented in the curriculum or represented in the teaching staff, because of the scores of ethnic and racial groups present today in every big city. It is an unrealistic and impossible demand for all to be represented. The answer from the multiculturalists could be that it may be unrealistic for all to be represented, but it is possible for the two largest ethnic groups of our big-city schools, blacks and Hispanics, to be represented, and after all it is their academic deficiency (and particularly that of blacks) which is the fundamental initiating cause of the entire debate.

Another debater's answer: The European immigrant child or the Asian child did not see himself in the curriculum or in his teachers, and yet he learned what was necessary. If the white Protestants taught the Irish, and the Irish taught the Jews and Italians, and the Jews and the Italians now teach the blacks and Hispanics, why is there a problem in the last term of this progression, and not in the preceding terms?

One counter answer would be that none of the learning of this type, by one immigrant group from teachers and textbooks that did not include them, was effective—that immigrants were poorly taught in the past, and the matter is the same (or for other reasons even worse) today when it comes to blacks and recent immigrant minorities. But that argument won't hold up to close scrutiny. Immigrants achieved incomes equivalent to that of natives in relatively short order, a decade or two according to some research, at worst in the next generation. The education of European immigrants, whatever depreciation of their culture and background they suffered in the schools, was far more effective than the education of black children has been, if measured by ability to gain economic equality. (Of course other factors aside from education kept blacks back.) So immigrants did not have to see themselves in the curriculum or among their teachers in order to succeed.

I once pointed out that those educated in the heyday of Americanization said, "We didn't need it, why do they? We didn't want it, why do they?" But I have come reluctantly to the conclusion that the position of blacks (and perhaps Hispanics, though there I would still resist the conclusion) is different from that of immigrants in some radical ways. While one can dispute the need for either the old immigrants or the new immigrants who now flood our schools to "see themselves in the curriculum," for blacks it is different.

Why? It would appear that the amount of "recognition" needed in the curriculum depends on the values, ideals, and conceptions students bring with them to school. If their ideal is "to become an American," the fact that the culture of their group and family is ignored in school may have no serious negative effects: Immigrants arrive at our borders, after all, with the intention of becoming Americanized. Most Asian immigrants, and many Hispanic immigrants (certainly Cubans, very likely Central Americans and South Americans, a good part of Mexicans) come today with the same hope. By contrast, the great majority of blacks are not immigrants or the children of immigrants, but are the descendants of slaves, and do not share the same experience or dreams. In grouping blacks together with recent non-European immigrants and their children, multiculturalism may be creating an amalgam that does not make sense for either population.

Groups can define themselves in various ways, and they have some degree of freedom in defining themselves. At one point blacks did define themselves as simply struggling for the same place in the United States that others had, achieved by the same means; the mark of success in their struggle would be that they would become no different from any other American except in color. At one time black leaders wanted exactly what existed for whites: assimilation into American society, culture, economy, and polity. That was, after all, the aim of school desegregation. This assimilationist ideal began to be rejected by blacks in the late 1960s, and eventually it changed among many other Americans as well.

▲ ▲ ▲

I think for the most part blacks define themselves differently today. Not to see themselves in the faculty, in the administrators, in the curriculum means to them that a condition of deprivation, of externally imposed inferiority, still exists. The counter arguments we could make—that blacks don't see teachers of their group because blacks are no longer interested in becoming teachers, or they can't pass the tests, or their place in the curriculum is the one that scholarly investigation properly has determined it should be, or the curriculum can't do it for everybody and no one group should receive special treatment—just won't wash.

Groups define themselves, nations define themselves, quite independently of how objective scholars, or scholars who believe themselves to be objective, think history and experience has defined them. Their self-definition is not simply a reflection of some objective reality. It is an expression of will. There is a good deal of myth and half-truth in these self-definitions, as we know from the history of nationalism. I think that a new process of self-definition is occurring among black Americans, but I say this with no great assurance. Perhaps I am too impressed by the more militant leaders and group advocates.

A sobering study by Terrie Epstein of the University of Michigan shows how divergent the perspectives of African American students may be from that of European American students. She conducted an intensive study of two eleventh-grade history classes in a midwestern urban high school, divided between African American and European American students. The students were asked who were the most important persons in American history, what were the most important events, and what sources did they trust most to get information on American history. The African American students rated Martin Luther King, Jr., Malcolm X, and Harriet Tubman the most important persons; the European American students listed George Washington, John F. Kennedy, and Martin Luther King, Jr. There was an equally striking difference on important events. The African American students chose the civil rights movement, the Civil War, and slavery and emancipation; the European Americans the Civil War, the Declaration of Independence, the Revolution. On credible sources in history, the African American students chose their family first, then the teacher, then TV, movies and video, and put the textbook in fourth place; the European American students chose the textbook first, the teacher second.

Based on interviews with the students, Professor Epstein concluded that "the European American students perceived a continuity in the historical perspectives they learned about at home, through the mainstream media, and at school, and rarely questioned the credibility of school-based information . . . The African American students . . . experienced a discontinuity in the historical perspectives they learned about at home and through alternative media programs, which resulted in skepticism and distrust of the history textbook . . . [They] also reported that their trust in teachers depended on the racial identity of the teacher and/or on the content and perspectives from which a teacher presented history."[6] How is one to deal with these radically different perspectives? One should realize that many black teachers will share the students' perspectives. (The teacher in these classes was white but seemed to have presented much material related to African American history.)

A range of approaches, some very different from multiculturalism, will be proposed by black educators and will work in black schools. Some programs emphasize Shakespeare, or algebra, instead of black studies, and they will succeed. Perhaps they will be more successful than Afrocentric or multicultural approaches. We don't know, because it is notoriously difficult to do convincing research on these matters. I would prefer Shakespeare and algebra for black students; I think it would do them and the nation more good. But the matter will have to be fought out politically. The decision will not be made unilaterally by those who believe Shake-speare and algebra are inherently better.

Is the issue that blacks need to see themselves in the teachers and texts to raise their self-esteem? What little evidence we have on the correlation between self-esteem and educational achievement is murky and inconclusive. On the negative side, the experience of Jews and Asians is devastating counter-evidence to the argument that a curriculum designed to enhance self-esteem is essential for learning. Further, blacks paradoxically generally show up in re-search as having as high or higher self-esteem than others, and yet their educational achievement is lower. Is this a kind of bravado, a cultural style, that in reality masks low self-esteem? It is well-known that American students think better of their performance in mathematics than Chinese or Japanese or Korean students, even though the Asians do better. Are we dealing with differences in cultural style or in some deep psychological characteristics when we see differences in self-esteem?[7]

Yet we should not rest there. It is indeed possible that for a group which has suffered experiences that have radically reduced self-respect, something to raise it—such as educational materials emphasizing group heroes and worthy role-models—might be helpful. Some evidence suggests that material related to African Americans does a better job in reaching these students. Ravitch and Finn in their study *What Do Our Seventeen-Year-Olds Know?* arrange the various items on which they tested students by the percentage from each race that got the right answers. On almost every question, more whites got the answer right than blacks. But then there were those few items on which blacks did better than whites. They were almost always items relating to black history and literature. So, more blacks than whites knew that the underground railway was a secret network to help slaves escape, that Harriet Tubman was a leader in its creation, that Martin Luther King, Jr., rose to prominence in the Montgomery bus boycott, that the

▲ ▲ ▲

Emancipation Proclamation freed the slaves in the Confederacy. On literature, more blacks than whites knew about King's "I have a dream" speech, about *The Red Badge of Courage, A Raisin in the Sun,* Langston Hughes, Ralph Ellison.[8] Perhaps they are more exposed to these materials in their schools. But black high school students do not on the whole attend schools in which they are in the overwhelming majority, as is common in elementary schools, and one would not expect the high school curriculum to be heavily weighted toward their interests.

The battle over the curriculum is most prominent in social studies and the humanities. It really can't get much of a hold in mathematics or science. In those fields, a few pleasing illusions or myths can be found, as in the Portland Baseline essays—background essays that were prepared for teachers in Portland, Oregon, to use to supplement the curriculum with information on black contributions, some of which are fantasy. But when it comes to the study of science and mathematics, the issue is not who discovered or invented what, and it doesn't much matter. The issue is: Can you solve the problem? Do you know how to get to an answer? Why does the experiment work?

The basic skills of reading and writing, calculating, being able to perform in mathematics and science are in the end the most important things to learn, certainly in the elementary grades. If a certain thrust in how we teach the humanities and the social sciences is associated with overall greater success in these crucial skills and capacities—and we don't know that it is—is that not a powerful argument in favor of multiculturalism? It would be, and perhaps in time we will come to some agreement that the Afrocentric curricula that are now being employed with many inner-city black students is doing them some good.

With the rise of charter schools and voucher plans and other forms of choice in public education, we will inevitably have more schools oriented toward black students and their needs. There has been a good deal of debate on the effects of the oldest public voucher plan in Milwaukee, where low-income black inner-city children have the opportunity to attend nonreligious private schools with public vouchers. The vouchers permit attendance only at schools with very modest fees, and these schools show various degrees of Afrocentrism. Apparently the children do no worse in these schools and may do better.[9]

In time, we will have more evidence on the matter of whether a curriculum sensitive to black students' interests and perspectives will achieve better educational results. Not that the evidence, in this educational initiative as in many others, is likely to be decisive: We will all stick to our preferences, which is what we do when we debate other curricular matters. Research doesn't decisively settle curricular debates because we can't do clinical tests, as we can with drugs, and therefore many other variables always come into the picture to help explain results. In the end, teachers and administrators and the larger forces of the culture, expressing themselves through the education of teachers and administrators, will decide.

4 ▲▲▲▲▲▲▲▲▲▲▲▲▲▲▲▲▲

THE REDISCOVERY OF
NUBIA AND KUSH

If one is guided by the intensity of the commentary from leading scholars, public figures, major organs of public opinion, then it is clear that the recent proposals for a greater degree of multicultural content in school and college curricula threaten to change, in some major and important ways, how we conduct our democracy and public affairs, how we live together in a common nation, how we manage a productive economy. In each case, the threat is one of divisiveness overcoming and superseding a healthy diversity. No one argues against diversity: neither Arthur Schlesinger, Jr., nor Diane Ravitch, nor the President of the American Federation of Teachers, Albert Shanker, nor the writers of cover stories for *Time* and *Newsweek*. But the critics do see a threat of disunity politically, of "fraying" culturally, of greater interethnic and interracial conflict among students and citizens generally.

More than national disunity and civil disharmony are involved, though these are central concerns (*The Disuniting of America*, according to Schlesinger, *The Fraying of America*, according to Robert Hughes). As we have seen, multiculturalism also questions our traditional stance toward truth in education, both how it is arrived

57

at and how it is taught. And equally important, it raises the issue of what makes any curriculum effective. We have struggled for thirty years or more with a substantial gap in the achievement of African American students, one not much reduced by efforts at school desegregation, increased funding for schools, or various types of educational reform. We also have a gap between major groups of Hispanic students—Mexicans, Puerto Ricans, and some others—and non-Hispanic whites. Multiculturalism has been offered as one way of reducing this gap, by engaging the interests of these students, by improving their self-esteem. The critics have responded that in raising self-esteem, multiculturalism substitutes what is irrelevant to education for what is relevant and necessary: achievement in reading, calculating, science, cultural literacy.

What posture is one to take toward this controversy? The historians, led by Ravitch and Schlesinger, who criticized the first New York State report, *A Curriculum of Inclusion,* said in effect that we should teach the truth, let the chips fall where they may. The historians' statement emphasized the autonomy and independence of history as a discipline establishing truths, and it criticized the committee that produced the first curriculum report because it included no historian. It insisted on the integrity of history as an intellectual discipline based on commonly accepted standards of evidence, but it also acknowledged at the same time that history has "shamefully neglected . . . the history of women, of immigrants, and of minorities."

Whether the distinguished signers really believed this last point I am not sure; the political realities made it necessary for them to say it in any case. Having made the necessary acknowledgment, they went on: "We have an equal commitment to standards of historical scholarship. We condemn the reduction of history to ethnic cheerleading on the demand of pressure groups." They then expressed a further concern: the "contemptuous" dismissal of the Western tradition by the New York State Committee. They acknowledged that "the West has committed its share of crimes against humanity, but the Western democratic philosophy also contains in its essence the means of exposing crimes and producing reforms." Finally, they asserted that "little can have more damaging effect on the republic than the use of the school system to promote the division of our people into antagonistic racial groups. We are after all a nation."

Clearly there are two souls struggling in this statement. One soul is that of commitment to historical truth as it is established at any given time by the body of professional historians, even though much remains disputed and controversial and the general body of agreements shifts over time. But the historians' statement cannot rest on truth alone. It also expresses concern over "the use of the school system to promote the division of our people into antagonistic racial groups." National unity is an eminently desirable objective, but what is its relationship to the primary objective of historical truth? Does it mean we will take into account in composing our truthful history whether some truths will promote divisiveness? (This was certainly a consideration in teaching history in the erstwhile Soviet Union and Yugoslav federation: presumably other truths are now taught in the successor states.)

Even in our democratic and open society, one can see how certain political objectives could lead us to emphasize or deemphasize various elements in our history. Do we insist on the self-corrective role of the Western liberal tradition, or do we accentuate the conflict, sometimes bloody conflict, and still continuing conflict, that has made for correction, often reluctant and forced? I know what I prefer: yes, acknowledge the crimes, but insist that most of that is behind us, that we live in a continuously improving society coming ever closer to the good society envisaged by our founding documents. I believe that is where the truth lies. I do not know how I would persuade someone who insists rather that there is still much to be done, that our freedoms and our equality are always in peril from malign forces, that the founding promise is still unrealized.

Thus even a statement in defense of the autonomy of historical truth (the *Newsday* reprint of this statement is headed "Don't Subject History to Political Revamping") has some political objectives, takes account of some political realities, in its rhetoric and its concessions. When it comes to the elementary and secondary schools, we have always had political, social, and moral objectives, and our teaching of history has never been free of them. We may personally prefer the history texts of the 1930s and '40s, with their strong narrative thrust, their emphasis on the main political line of American history, their celebration of the virtues and triumphs of American society and polity, their very modest attention, if any, to current issues of race. But a good deal has happened since then. The issues of class debated by the historians of the 1930s and '40s have found their way into history texts; the story of immigration plays a somewhat larger role; we pay much, much greater attention to women, and of course we pay much greater attention to race.

Only under the rubric of Global Studies do high school students in New York State get any European history at all nowadays, and even so they don't get much of it: All of Europe, past and present, is taken up in something like a seventh of the one-year curriculum in Global Studies. The curriculum syllabus for Global Studies our social studies review committee saw (see Chapter 2) was organized to give equal time to Africa, East Asia, Europe, Latin America, the Middle East, South Asia, and the Soviet world. (Presumably there has been some revision since the collapse of the Soviet Empire.)

I prefer what I got in high school: a full year of European history (Asia and Africa got in under the treatment of imperialism, colonialism, and the causes of World War I). But I don't see how I will persuade those who are convinced that the older curriculum was retrograde, disrespectful of minorities, women, and the Third World. I also prefer the consensual nature of the history I got: I think it was better for the country, better for me. At the time, if multicultural studies had been in effect, the Jews would have learned how anti-Semitic America was, the Italians how anti-Italian. Under the circumstances, we got that at home. Was that better or worse?

How does one demonstrate that consensus and harmony have played a larger role in American history than conflict and dissent, or really any other major central issue in American history that is disputed in arguments over curriculum? Of course the determination of what should be taught in history must take account of scholarship, must not teach falsehoods, but to some extent political objectives will determine the history we prefer, and different groups will have different political objectives.

History is becoming much more of a battleground today than it once was, and there are many reasons for this aside from multiculturalism. One is the rise of a new history—of immigrants, of minorities, of women, of gays and lesbians. One looks at these new trends at their beginning with bemusement, but in time they become part of established history, with their classics, their programs, their professors, their texts. These trends begin in anger but end in scholarship and incorporation into college curricula. In time, they begin to influence high school history.

Another sturdy root of multiculturalism is the generally greater sophistication with which we view the role of the United States in the world. It is not God's country anymore. We can lose wars, as in Vietnam, we can be beaten in economic competition by the Japanese, we can become only one of a number of economically powerful, democratic countries, and one not in every respect the best. To insist otherwise seems retrograde.

A third pillar of multiculturalism is the larger reality of the non-Western world. A good deal of it is sunk in poverty and political disorder, but some of it is teaching lessons in economic effectiveness to the West. Western hubris can never again be what it was in the late nineteenth and early twentieth century. And American hubris can never be what it was when the United States alone produced half the measured income in the world. Our production is now down to a fifth, and it is reasonable for that change in world status to be reflected in school curricula.

A fourth contributor to a multiculturalist worldview is the shaking of confidence in science and irreversible progress. A fifth is the decline in religious faith in the West. And we could think of others, all of which make it impossible to teach history simply as a progress, with the United States standing at its apex.

There is more debunking, of more kinds, than there used to be—and we should all remember that debunking is an old American word. In time all these trends must affect the teaching of history at the elementary and high school levels. It is not only multiculturalism or Afrocentrism that is changing scholarship and teaching in history, and it would give these movements too great credit to attribute the changes history teaching is undergoing solely to them.

In an age of dissensus in which the authority of teachers and administrators is much reduced, one cannot escape the role of politics when we come to curriculum reform. In the lower schools, the teaching of history is in any case always something more than the teaching of the truth as established by the consensus of scholarship, and I don't see how we can escape that. Truth, as the discipline establishes it, will play a role in this political solution. But it will be disputed, and politically there will be no way of ruling those who dispute it out of court. On the committees that represent teachers and principals and community leaders, we will listen respectfully a good deal of the time to what will strike us as nonsense. But note that even the most extreme of the multiculturalists insist that what drives them is also the search for the truth, a suppressed truth. Some of them argued that the first report should have been labeled not *A Curriculum of Inclusion* but *A Curriculum of Truth*.

In the course of the conflict over the New York State curriculum, I reviewed California's social studies curriculum revision, which appeared at the time to be a much more harmonious and successful effort at reform. It was entitled *History–Social Sciences Framework for California Public Schools, Kindergarten through Grade Twelve*, and it had been carried through with deliberation and care by a highly professional group that included Diane Ravitch. Its major substantive goal is given as "Democratic Understanding and Civic Values," and the first specification under that goal is "National Identity." The framework reads:

> To understand this nation's identity, students must: Recognize that American identity is now and has always been pluralistic and multicultural. From the first encounter between indigenous peoples and exploring Europeans, the inhabitants of the North American continent have represented a variety of races, religions, languages, and ethnic and racial groups. With the passage of time, the United States has grown increasingly diverse in its social and cultural composition. Yet, even as our people have become increasingly diverse, there is broad recognition we are one people. Whatever our origins, we are all Americans.

The first subtheme under "National Identity" is: "Understand the American creed as extolling equality and freedom." The only individual quoted under this theme (or indeed in the entire section on national identity) is Martin Luther King, Jr. The subsequent subthemes call for the curriculum to "Recognize the status of minorities and women in different times in American history; Understand the unique experiences of immigrants from Asia, the Pacific Islands, and Latin America; Understand the special role of the United States in world history as a nation for immigrants; Realize that true patriotism celebrates the moral force of the American idea of nation that unites as one people the descendants of many cultures, races, religions, and ethnic groups." Multiculturalism seems prominent even in a curriculum proposal that, I assume, would have gained the approval of the historians who signed the statement attacking *A Curriculum of Inclusion.*

The major thrust of the generally admired California *History–Social Science Framework* was to place greater emphasis on narrative history, as against a fuzzy social studies and social problems emphasis (the kind of thing that unfortunately infects New York State's Global Studies), to emphasize positive features in American history, and to reinstate the historical role of America's various religions, which had been banned from the curriculum previously in an excessively cautious effort to comply with the Constitutional requirement of separation of church and state.

The California framework was applauded widely, but there were a few attacks. Catherine Cornbleth and Dexter Waugh, who have studied both the California and the New York conflicts, found the framework inadequate: "California's version of American history was based on an immigrant perspective that in effect subjugated Native Americans, African Americans, and former Mexican citizens in the Southwest to the status of ride-alongs, rather than primary participants and shapers of America's dynamic, hybrid culture." They quote Joyce E. King, an education professor of Santa Clara University "who fought a losing battle against California's brand of modest multiculturalism while a member of California's state Curriculum Commission," as saying: "They put everyone in the covered wagon." Indians, Mexicans, Chinese, and blacks had not gotten to California that way. And to another critic, Sylvia Wynter, in the departments of African and Afro-American Studies and Spanish and Portuguese at Stanford, California's multicultural curriculum "promotes a culturally pluralistic version of American society downplaying, if not ignoring, its racial and cultural hierarchy. California's version of history functioned to represent Euro-immigrant America as the 'universally valid perspective of all America.'"[1] This is to Cornbleth and Waugh "additive" or "revisionist" multiculturalism, not "transformative" multiculturalism.

This criticism from the left was scattered, and the California State Board of Education accepted a set of textbooks which had been produced in response to the framework. Compared with the initial (relative) harmony around the adoption of the framework, the textbooks aroused storms of controversy. They were denounced as being inadequate in their treatment of the history and character of various religions and racial and ethnic groups, and they were rejected by the one large California city that is dominantly black, Oakland. The criticism was not only from blacks: Jews protested the description of the Hebrew Bible as the "Old Testament" and objected to the fact that Jewish history, as far as the textbooks were concerned, seemed to end with the rise of Christianity. In a textbook series laden with images and typographical gimmicks, Muslims objected to the use of a camel to stand as a symbol for Islam. The effort to bring religion back into the American history classroom was not universally approved.

The California story is worth pondering for at least two reasons. The first is that even the most balanced and professional effort to define a curriculum for students in American schools today will place a heavy emphasis on multiplicity and diversity, race and ethnicity. That is our reality today. While there are many differences between the California framework and the second New York State report, *One Nation, Many Peoples,* a Martian, or a Frenchman, would be impressed by the similarities. And a second reason the story is exemplary is this: Whatever efforts we make to include all the strands that constitute American society, we will not, in the present state of affairs, avoid conflict altogether. The California texts—responding as they did to the call for inclusion of ethnic and religious minorities, reaching beyond the central story of American history as presented in previous texts, taking in much more of world history sympathetically—were rejected by some cities and attacked in almost all. Achieving consensus on textbooks in history is not easy.

▲ ▲ ▲

These lessons have been further emphasized in the most recent conflict over multiculturalism, this time the debate over national standards for teaching American and world history. One important thrust in our efforts since the early 1980s to improve American education has been the attempt to create national standards in the major subjects taught in schools. These standards would serve to tell state education departments, school boards, teachers, principals, textbook publishers, and test makers what an authoritative and widely representative group of experts believes should be included in the teaching of mathematics, science, literature, history, and the like. While there is great similarity in American schools, and on the whole students will not be too surprised moving from state to state at what is included in the teaching of the different grades, there is no authoritative source for what should be covered. Our federal Department of Education has no authority, as do the education ministries in Japan and France and some other countries, to establish curriculum.

The effort to produce national standards has been difficult and tortured.[2] Many Americans are suspicious of the Department of Education, fearing it will try to take over the functions of state agencies or local boards of education. Nevertheless, the effort has gone forward. Following the American pattern, the standards will be models, with no authority unless states or local boards adopt them or make use of them in some respect. But their advocates hope they will serve as first steps in informing students, parents, teachers, principals, and state officials what a desirable curriculum should be. As is the case with curricula generally, it is pretty clear what should be done in mathematics, but as one moves toward subjects like English literature and history, things become more complicated.

Those responsible for the generally admired California framework were chosen to undertake the same job for national standards in history. Funds were provided to UCLA's National Center for

History in the Schools, headed by Charlotte Crabtree (who had been in charge of creating the California framework) and Gary Nash (who had been one of the authors of the history textbooks created in response to it), by the National Endowment for the Humanities, then headed by Lynne Cheney, and by the Office of Educational Research and Innovation of the Department of Education, then headed by Diane Ravitch. A National Council for History Standards was set up to oversee the process, and among the leading scholars on this council one will find no strident voice for multiculturalism, and a number of persons who could be expected to be critical if the standards became too trendy and fashionable.

For example, Kenneth Jackson of Columbia University, who criticized the second New York State report, *One Nation, Many Peoples*, was on the Council. Bernard Lewis, a Middle Eastern scholar who is regularly attacked as an example of Western arrogance toward the Muslim world, and Elizabeth Fox-Genovese, a critic of extreme feminism, were members. Also serving were many other scholars of distinction who, it could be expected, would not be apologists for multiculturalism—Ainslee Embree and Carol Gluck of Columbia, William McNeill of Chicago, Akira Iriye of Harvard, Morton Keller of Brandeis. Gilbert Sewall, director of the American Textbook Council and a critic of textbooks that reach too far in a multicultural direction, was also on the Council. It was a list that would certainly have made the advocates of transformative multiculturalism unhappy.

This was only the peak body involved, and it may have been only distantly involved. The process of creating the history standards displayed a remarkable inclusiveness. There were scores of participating organizations: the American Historical Association and the Organization of American Historians; many associations dealing with social studies education; major school reform groups; associations of administrators; groups concerned with the history of one group or one religion: the National Alliance of Black School Educators; the National Association for Asian and Pacific American Education; the Council for Islamic Education; the League of United Latin American Citizens. Task forces, forums, and focus groups were formed. It was an elaborate process indeed, leading to three volumes published at the end of 1994, one for standards from kindergarten through fourth grade and two for standards from fifth grade through high school, for American history and world history.

They evoked an immediate windstorm of criticism, led by Lynne Cheney in the *Wall Street Journal.* There was in these volumes apparently no mention of great American heroes such as Paul Revere and Thomas Edison, Alexander Graham Bell or the Wright brothers, but Harriet Tubman rated six mentions, Senator McCarthy and McCarthyism were cited 19 times, the Great Depression 25 times. And the Ku Klux Klan was prominently featured.[3] The criticism reverberated and was picked up in talk shows and in op-ed page pieces everywhere. The United States Senate denounced the standards in a 99 to 1 vote. The senator who cast the lone vote against the resolution later explained he had misunderstood it, and meant to denounce the history standards too.

There was much in the volumes that would have struck any reader as odd indeed: the emphasis given to the history of pre-literate Mexican and African societies about which we know almost nothing; the presence of aspects of Asian and African history known only to specialists but now expected to be absorbed by elementary and high school students; the emphasis on the role of women in every era of world history, and in every phase of American history. One wondered what specialists, let alone fifth graders or high school students, could know about "gender roles" in pre-Columbian Indian societies or in the earliest agricultural communities of the Middle East. Yet this was something the student was expected to discourse on. There was a remarkable neutrality in discussing the Cold War. And much else was open to criticism.

Also, undoubtedly, much was admirable, in particular the "Standards in Historical Thinking," which called, among other things, for teaching students how to think chronologically, and how to think about historical evidence. But overall, multiple perspectives were clearly in the saddle.[4]

The standards could not withstand this political storm, and a process of revision was undertaken. Panels appointed by the conservative Council for Basic Education played an important role in this revision. Once again, the review panels included people who could be expected to cast a cold eye on multicultural excess — Ravitch, Stephen Thernstrom, David Hollinger, and Maris Vinovskis, among others. The new standards emerged, their bulk stripped down by the elimination of the teaching examples, where some of the more egregious cases cited by the critics had occurred. How could anything go wrong now, after two processes overseen by critical and objective historians?

But the revised and improved standards were also denounced. "New History Standards Still Attack Our Heritage," wrote Lynne Cheney in the *Wall Street Journal.*[5] "History Standards Get It Wrong Again," wrote John Patrick Diggins in the *New York Times.*[6] Cheney did not have as vivid examples as she was able to provide in her attack on the first version of the standards, but she objected to the assertion that the American Revolution "called into question" the relationships between man and woman and parent and child, that the Great Depression ranks with the American Revolution in "its effects on the lives of Americans," that "at the beginning of the twentieth century Western nations enjoyed a dominance they no longer possess." (The quoted passages are from the standards.) I see no smoking guns there.

Diggins presented a stronger case. Once again we are startled by the recovery of figures known hitherto mostly to specialists. Students are asked: "Appraise the survival strategies employed by Native Americans such as Speckled Snake, Red Eagle, Sequoyah,

Tenskawatawa, Tecumseh, Osceola, and Black Hawk." Diggins writes: "The standards still rest on assumptions that are dubious if not preposterous. The most glaring contradiction is that its authors seek to inculcate political values characteristic of the Western World that cannot be derived from what they would have students learn about the non-Western world."

This strikes me, as a reader of the standards, as quite true. One of the values the standards want to expose students to is tolerance and respect for others, but these qualities are hard to find in the practice of human sacrifice in Mayan and Aztec society or in the absence of anything like democracy or constitutional rule in almost all non-Western and non-European societies before the impact of the West. The standards drag out of the murkiest recesses of history—as long as these recesses are non-European—peoples hardly known, perhaps of impressive accomplishments in stone sculpture or architecture, and they raise these up alongside the greatest and most creative epochs of human history.

Diggins strikes perhaps his strongest blow against the United States history standards by citing how they start off the nation's history: Students are told that at the very beginning of the history of the land that eventually became the United States and the people that eventually became the Americans, as that term is commonly understood, is the "historical convergence of European, African, and Native American people." An intriguing perspective certainly. Some decades ago, if asked what convergence of what peoples shaped or created the American people, one might, in the darkness of those days, have ventured the English, the Spanish, and the French. These are now all subsumed in "Western European societies" and together given no greater place in the standards than West African and Native American societies.

One problem in this replacement for the teaching of history is that we know a great deal about Western Europe, and we know comparatively so little about West African and Native American

▲ ▲ ▲

societies before the coming of the Europeans. The efforts of archaeologists and historians have recovered a good deal, but it is still asking a lot of students to expect them to "explain the common elements of Native American societies such as gender roles, family organization, religion, and values and compare their diversity in languages, shelter, labor systems, political structures, and economic organization," or to "describe general features of family organization, labor division, agriculture, manufacturing and trade in Western African societies." All these tasks have to be done for the fifteenth century, and there still remains a year of American history to go.⁷ Such questions would probably be too much to ask for even Western Europe, but the standards are nothing if not ambitious. One suspects that their teachers would have no inkling of how to go about teaching students these things. Whatever the situation in the past, the student of today will certainly be alerted to "gender roles" in any society or period, even if archaeologists and historians do not have much to say about the matter yet.

The world history standards, in their multicultural thrust, raise more difficult questions for me than the American history standards. Whatever the originality of the convergence of the three peoples as a way of starting American history, Native Americans and Africans have played a substantial role in our common subsequent history, politically, culturally, economically. The need for "equal respect" leads to rather odder results in world history.

One is the recovery of the history of Nubia and Kush, areas south of Egypt, influenced by Egypt, but hitherto in the wings as far as Egyptian history is concerned. No longer. This area of Africa is now thrust into the center of the stage. One cannot help but believe that the reason for this prominence is that otherwise sub-Saharan Africa would play too little a role in world history for too long a time. So, for the era 4000 to 1000 BCE, which focuses on the early civilizations of Mesopotamia, Egypt, and the Indus Valley, students are asked to "assess the importance of commercial, cultural, and political connections between Egypt and the peoples of Nubia along the upper Nile."8 For the same period, they are asked to "analyze evidence for the growth of agricultural societies in tropical West Africa . . . in the second millennium BCE."9

In the next era, "Classical Traditions, Major Religions, and Giant Empires, 1000 BCE–300 CE," we find for the first part of that period, 1000 to 600 BCE, alongside sections on the Mediterranean and Southwest Asia (iron-making, Assyrian and New Babylonian empires, Phoenician trade, emergence of Greek city-states, spread of alphabetic writing) and the emergence of Judaism and the historical significance of the Hebrew Kingdoms, a section on the states of the upper Nile valley. The student is supposed to be able to "assess the importance of political, commercial, and cultural relations between Egypt and Nubia/Kush"; "analyze the effects of Nile trade and the decline of the New Kingdom as factors in the power of Kush in the first millennium BCE"; "evaluate the linguistic, architectural, and artistic achievements of Kush in the Meroitic period"; "analyze how Kushite and Assyrian invasions affected Egyptian society"; "explain connections between maritime trade and the power of the kingdom of Aksum in Northeast Africa"; "describe the emergence of states south of the Sahara desert and appraise theories of how iron-working technology spread in West and East Africa."10 Egypt has by now been quite swallowed up by Nubia/Kush.11

Nor are the Native Americans neglected. For the period 500 BCE to 300 CE, alongside Standard 3, "How major religious and large-scale empires arose in the Mediterranean basin, China, and India," which covers the Roman Empire, Christianity, the early Chinese imperial dynasties, and India, we find the parallel (and meant to be equally significant?) Standard 4, "The development of early agrarian civilizations in Mesoamerica." In this standard the student is expected to "interpret archaeological evidence for the development of Olmec civilization in the second and first millennium BCE";

"evaluate major Olmec contributions to . . . the calendar, glyphic writing, sculpture and monumental building"; and "assess Olmec cultural influence on the emergence of civilization in the Oaxaca valley and other regions."[12]

As a history buff, I find all this fascinating, as I do the detail on Chinese history, where, for example, the student will learn about every major Chinese dynasty, and will learn (twice, indeed) about the voyages of the Chinese admiral Zheng He in the fifteenth century. (The names of Vasco Da Gama, Magellan, and Columbus, do not appear, perhaps on the assumption that of course the teachers would bring them in?) But there is an issue of proportionality, of judgment as to the weighty and the less weighty in history, to be made, and two things have obscured proper judgment. One is the role of historical specialists, who understandably want students to know more about areas of the world they consider important and that have been neglected. Further, they are aware of, and have participated in, the changes in the practice of history that reduce the significance of political history, increase the importance of social history, of the history of science and technology, of the role of gender in history, of history from below generally, and they want to bring all this in.[13] But the second factor is certainly political: Africa must get into the story, and must parallel Egypt and classical civilization, and the indigenous peoples of the New World must get into the story, as ancestors of today's Native Americans but perhaps more important as ancestors also of our second largest minority, Hispanic Americans.

There seems to be no escape from multiculturalism, even when the effort to create standards in history is financed by those well aware of its potential dangers and occasional excesses, and even when scholars with similar concerns are involved in the process. We are all expected to defer to multiculturalism today.

Meanwhile, the process of creating a new curriculum in social studies for New York State has been continuing all these years, with various committees working away and trying to come to some consensus. The process is in some respects coming to an end. Standards have been approved by the Board of Regents of the State of New York in a variety of fields, including social studies. No one is very happy with the social studies standards: "The AFT [American Federation of Teachers] considers the state's . . . social studies standards unacceptable. Many reviewers would not argue with the union's evaluation of the social studies standards, which have been mired in controversy since 1987. Regardless of political persuasion, those who have reviewed the final document say the social studies standards are so lacking in substance that they are virtually useless."[14]

No one could disagree. In an effort probably to avoid controversy and achieve what consensus is possible, the standards are reduced and thinned out, and say very little. But I note with interest that Kush has made it into these very brief and minimal standards: The elementary school student is expected to "analyze pictures and maps of the civilizations of Kush and Egypt including information about their architectural, artistic, and technological achievements," and "study about the major cultural achievements of an ancient civilization (e.g., West African, Japanese, Chinese, European)." Similarly with the "intermediate" student, who is "to investigate the important achievements . . . of the world's early civilizations (e.g., African, Greek, Roman, Egyptian, Indian, Chinese)." The advanced ("Commencement") student will also not neglect Africa. Among the "important turning points and developments in world history" he is asked to investigate are "the Mali Empire in West Africa," which appears in a list of key turning-points, sandwiched between the Mongol Empire and the Age of Exploration.[15]

The key issue here for critics confronting this apparent irresistibility of multiculturalism is this: What is the underlying purpose of these curriculum reforms? Is it to promote harmony and the acceptance of our society as good and fair; to include the excluded? Or is it to promote a view of our society as fatally flawed by racism, irredeemably unfair and unequal, and thus to be rejected as evil? Is the United States the fundamentally decent and good society that America is for so many, or is it the "Amerika" ("k" standing for the Ku Klux Klan and the German spelling of America) denounced by the radicals and racial militants of the late 1960s and '70s?

The critics of multiculturalism fear that it is the second vision which underlies the strong multicultural position. In part, they are right: such a vision of our country does motivate some multiculturalists. But if we look further into the objectives of most of those who promote a strong multicultural thrust, and who in doing so present a somewhat lopsided view of our history, we will find that they promote it, for the most part, not because they aim at divisiveness and separatism as a good, not because they want to break up the union, but because they aim at a fuller inclusiveness of deprived groups. Proximately, their vision may well mean more conflict and divisiveness, but they see this as a stage to a greater inclusiveness. They are no Quebec separatists, Croatian nationalists, Sikh or Tamil separatists. They seek inclusion and equality in a common society. Their view of the principles that should govern this equality may be disputed, but that brings us to such issues as affirmative action, ethnic studies, and yes, multiculturalism, not to issues of fundamental and irreconcilable division of the kind we have faced in the past, and that so many countries face today.

We are quite far in the present dispute from the naive and unrealistic separatists of the late 1960s and '70s. It is frustration at the failure to bring a larger share of blacks into the common society that drives multiculturalism today. This may appear—I know it will—to the critics of the new multiculturalism as a far too benign judgment as to the underlying intentions of its proponents, and its possible effects. I view these trends in the context of the alarm over disunity that they have aroused, and perhaps I take too extreme an outcome (civil war among ethnic and racial groups?) as a test against which to estimate their effects. One can think of lesser effects that are serious enough: for example, greater hostility between blacks and whites, and among other ethnic and racial groups. But I do not think this hostility, which was evident long before any element of multiculturalism affected school curricula, is the result of a multicultural curriculum. We should not exaggerate the effects of the content of teaching in history and the humanities. Were Americans better patriots when Lincoln and Washington were on the school walls instead of Martin Luther King, Jr., and Cesar Chavez, and if they were, was it for that reason?

Undoubtedly one can point to some outspoken black leaders in multiculturalism whose intentions are not benign. Leonard Jeffries, Jr., for example, accentuates the split between Jews and blacks, teaches a racial interpretation of history, reviving nineteenth-century racist anthropology, and propagates outlandish views and illusions as truth. He stands at one extreme. Less extravagant views attract numerous followers in the world of education, some supporting them out of a misguided position that anything to enhance the self-image of blacks is a good thing, others giving support out of white guilt over the condition of blacks, and others, among blacks, supporting them because they honestly believe the Afrocentrists have a superior truth. All this is often associated with the conviction that "they"—the hidden powers—are plotting to destroy blacks through drugs and AIDS, a point of view that is alarmingly widespread among the black population. These views must be fought—the racial interpretation, the extravagant enhancement of the role of black Africa in world history, the belief in malevolent plots and conspiracies. On this last point, I am not confident about what even vigorous denunciation can do. Consider that among educated and uneducated whites (as well as blacks), we have not done very well in affecting the widespread view that some vast conspiracy lies behind the assassination of John F. Kennedy. Why wouldn't many blacks believe the same about the assassinations of Malcolm X and Martin Luther King, Jr.?

But I would reemphasize that we deal with a spectrum of views in multiculturalism, some reasonable enough to gain the endorsement of Ravitch, Schlesinger, and Shanker, and some extreme enough to be endorsed by Asa Hilliard III and Jeffries. In the middle there is a good deal to argue about, as to both content and effectiveness of presentation. We should also bear in mind that although parents are not usually enthusiasts of multicultural education, they are ready to try almost anything—uniforms, schools for black boys, Afrocentric curricula, schools of choice—to improve the achievement of their children in school. Those who oppose these trends will not be the parents of the children in the schools, or the teachers in the classrooms, or even in many places a majority of the voters. They will be an elite telling the big-city school leaders what they should do for the good of the country and in order to be faithful to the truths of history. These professional historians and philosophers of education will get a great deal of media attention for their views, but in the end they will not, I think, win on the ground.

5 ▲▲▲▲▲▲▲▲▲▲▲▲▲▲▲▲

DEALING WITH
DIVERSITY, PAST
AND PRESENT

Multiculturalism, whatever it is or will be, seems to arise from some sea change in values affecting a large segment of the educational profession, as well as many academics and intellectuals in the humanities and social sciences. It raises the general question of how we are to understand our nation and its culture. What monuments are we to raise (or raze), what holidays are we to celebrate, how are we to name our schools and our streets? The 400th anniversary of Columbus's voyage (once a "discovery," now an "encounter," or something less neutral) was a great national holiday, culminating in our greatest World's Fair in Chicago in 1893. The 500th anniversary was a conflict-ridden and muted affair in which nothing much happened, or was allowed to happen, aside from a spate of books denouncing Columbus.

How do we memorialize great events or noteworthy individuals? A statue depicting Friar Junipero Serra and a Spanish Conquistador, with a grateful or humble or submissive Indian at their feet, was moved from a prominent location in San Francisco for some construction project. Should it be moved back? Moved to a less prominent spot? Put in storage? We have long argued over the

▲ ▲ ▲

appropriateness of Christmas creches and Hanukkah celebrations in public spaces. Traditionally these arguments have centered around issues of separation of church and state, but an increasingly multicultural society will identify new issues. One can well imagine that in cities with large black populations the question will be raised of the race of the figures shown, or whether the display should not rather celebrate Kwanza, an emerging African American holiday meant to compete with a white Christmas.

We have seen cases in sports where the argument has been over whether a player may wear a yarmulke, and in the police or in the army over whether a Sikh can wear a turban. These come to the courts because of the Constitutional protection of religion, and could not get to the courts as cultural differences because culture does not receive the same protection in the Constitution as religion, but they are inherently issues of culture.

This changing understanding of our nation, its history, its values, its faults has important policy consequences beyond the symbolic, for example, in immigration policy. One of the most striking changes of the recent past has been the increasing acceptance of pluralism as a central American value—the acceptance of all races, both sexes, different lifestyles as being equally good and deserving of respect and of protection against discrimination—and we see this at work in the nondiscriminatory immigration policy that has been in effect for thirty years. Even the changes in immigration policy debated and instituted in 1996 did not raise overtly the issue of changing the ethnic and racial composition of immigrants, a striking fact in view of the sharp divergence between the ethnic and racial composition of immigrants today and the ethnic and racial composition of the American population. One does occasionally find the (somewhat repressed) attitude that the United States should remain primarily a white, or Christian, or Anglo-Saxon, nation, but the arguments over our immigration policy still are couched primarily in pluralistic terms: Those who object to the present scale of immigration are careful to emphasize that they have no argument with its racial and ethnic mix, so different from the prevailing dominance of white Europeans in the population of the United States, but that they are concerned rather with the number of illegal immigrants, or the costs imposed on local and state government, or the competition for jobs between legal and illegal immigrants and native Americans, or between earlier immigrants and later legal immigrants. How long this obeisance to the values of pluralism and universalism, the refusal to make distinctions by race and ethnicity, will prevail is uncertain.

Multiculturalism raises its head in politics, but not in so many words. Two large groups, blacks and Hispanics, and some smaller groups, Asians and Native Americans, receive special protection under the Voting Rights Act, and this special protection has led, in the wake of the 1990 census, to the creation of fantastically shaped districts, in an effort to satisfy Justice Department requirements for districts with majorities of minorities sufficient to elect a minority representative. Multiculturalism raises its head in the inner life of political parties, particularly the Democratic Party, which has struggled now for decades with the rules governing minority-group representation in national conventions.

On the local level, it is a rare political issue that does not have racial and group implications these days. What services should be cut? What voluntary agencies should provide them? What areas should lose firehouses or food-distribution centers? These issues are often cast starkly in black-white terms, but almost as commonly in black-white-Hispanic terms, and sometimes other groups are involved, such as Chinese in lower Manhattan seeking a district in which they might elect one of their own, or Hasidic Jews arguing for a greater allotment of public housing or more police protection. Are these "multicultural" issues? Are they even in any serious sense *cultural* issues? Certainly they concern groups with a specific cultural character, but the groups mobilize and make demands less to defend cultural values than to defend jobs, or representation, or entitlements, or property. But then it can be argued that jobs, representation, entitlements, and property do serve to protect cultural values.

All these issues raise the questions: Who are we as Americans? What kind of nation do we want? How are we to live together? What claims does any common or normative culture legitimately make on those who are marked by a variety of cultural differences? And these questions come up most strongly in education. There, multiculturalism has spread to encompass almost every issue, some of which are quite distinct from questions of curriculum.

Not the least of these is the persisting problem of segregation — the concentration of black and Hispanic students in central city schools — a problem with which we have struggled now for more than forty years. By itself, changing the racial mix of students need have no effect on curriculum or on the culture of school and college, and in that respect it is quite different from the issues we think of under the rubric of multiculturalism. The massive change in school populations caused by the huge migrations from Europe in the late nineteenth and early twentieth centuries had surprisingly little effect on curriculum, aside perhaps from spurring the rise of vocational education. Similarly, when we set out decades ago on the effort to racially desegregate our schools, it was not expected, by black or white, that one consequence of desegregation would be a massive change in curriculum. Blacks then hoped to have schools just like whites, in facilities, in finances, in textbooks, in curricula, in achievement, and the same was true in the first efforts to integrate colleges. Today we know that changing the mix of students did have consequences for curricula, but that is because other changes were occurring simultaneously in the culture which made the students of the ever more diverse schools and colleges (and their advocates) very different from the students of the age of mass immigration, or of the first decade or two of school desegregation.

Multiculturalism today is also entwined with the issues raised by the selection, placement, and promotion of staff, teachers, and principals, that is, the gamut of issues raised by affirmative action and the drive for "diversity." Just as in the case of the changing mix of students, a changing mix of teachers and administrators did have consequences for curriculum, but it need not have been so. The introduction of large numbers of Irish and German, then Jewish and Italian teachers and principals into New York City public schools had almost no impact on curriculum. (Italian and Jewish educators did argue for adding Italian and modern Hebrew to the foreign languages taught in high school.) The introduction of more black teachers and administrators, in an environment different from that of the last few decades, might have had as little consequence. But in the context of the 1980s and '90s, more black and other minority teachers and administrators did mean more pressure for multiculturalism in the curriculum.

School and college administrators seek today for more black teachers and administrators because of pressure from students and some government agencies, because they accept the basic justice of such efforts, or because they think this will be good for black students, rather than because they expect or want the greater number of minority teachers and administrators to change the way the school and college go about their business. But greater numbers of black teachers and administrators will do more than serve as an example of the search for justice and equity, or as role models for students. Even if they have no strong intention of changing curriculum and school and college atmosphere, the mere fact they are black, raised in a somewhat different setting and culture, will make them different from white teachers. They may be more understanding of black students, or alternatively stricter and more demanding, but how they act will stem from some interaction between their background and how they see and respond to black students. This change in teachers may have no necessary impact on curriculum, and in many cases it does not, but in today's world it will very likely change what is taught.

The rules under which schools operate, in particular issues of discipline, raise questions of culture, and multiculturalism, too. When is student behavior to be considered disobedient, or impertinent, or disruptive, and what is one to do about it? These are among the chief multicultural issues in schools today, often dividing minority students and their parents from white administrators and teachers. But they are different from the issues raised by the rewriting of curricula and the creation of new guidelines for textbooks.

Certain objectives of education are not much in dispute: higher educational achievement for all groups, a measure of civil harmony, competence in performing the tasks that are basic to economic productivity. All of these require other qualities such as truthfulness, responsibility, ability to communicate, and all are the common objectives of both multiculturalists and their opponents. But, as we have seen, how to achieve these objectives is the question that divides many advocates of multiculturalism from their opponents.

The new multicultural thrust in the colleges and universities has received the lion's share of media attention. The replacement of a required Western Civilization course at Stanford by somewhat different courses with a focus on minorities, Third World peoples, and women was perhaps the first widely reported major battle in the multicultural wars. In retrospect, the changes demanded were fairly mild. Greater changes were soon on the way: the establishment of required courses on American minorities at the University of California, Berkeley, at the University of Minnesota, at Hunter College, and elsewhere; sit-ins in many institutions by students demanding more black and Hispanic faculty and more black and Hispanic studies (and, on occasion, more Asian American studies).

The situation is more serious, however, in elementary and secondary public schools. There the issue is not, shall we have an ethnic studies program (in which few students will choose to specialize), or shall we have a required course on race and ethnicity (which students will take with some grumbling, and many of which will be not very different from courses they might have taken anyway). The issue in public education is rather, what shall be the content of *required* courses that *all* students must take and be tested on and that will make up their *entire* education in social studies and history and literature. In the colleges, presumably, there will always be courses in American and European and Asian and African history that are not affected by the political pressures stemming from America's racial situation. But the question is, will such an education be possible, or survive, in the public schools in the wake of multicultural demands? That was the issue in New York State.

Multiculturalism looks like something very new in American public education, and in many respects it is. Yet in other ways it is a new word for an old problem: how public education is to respond to and take account of the diversity of backgrounds of public school students, religious, ethnic, racial. Public education in the United States, at least that part of it in our major cities, has never been free of this issue since its origins in the 1840s, when the first of the "great school wars," as Diane Ravitch calls them in her history of New York City public schools, broke out.[1] It centered on the demands of Catholic leaders for something like equal treatment for Catholic students. Urban public education had been the creation of reformers with a Protestant religious background; and, as historians have pointed out, one of their principal aims was the socialization of children into the Protestant moral and religious world of the mid-nineteenth century. They did not think of this as anything distinctively sectarian or parochial: That world was accepted without question as the way things should be in America.

Catholic religious leaders, on the other hand, objected. In particular they resisted readings from the Protestant King James Bible. No one dreamed, in those distant days, that the First

Amendment to the Constitution, with its prohibition of any "establishment of religion," would in time be used to ban *all* Bible reading in schools, or even a moment of silence, if its motivation had some taint of religion about it. The outcome of the conflict was that Catholics decided to establish their own schools, to the degree their capacities allowed, and they created a separate, Catholic system of education in the major cities of the country, apart from the public school system.

In the 1880s and '90s, we again find major public school disputes that we would call "multicultural" today, but this time centering on the rights of German children to receive instruction in German. Teaching in German was widely established in Cincinnati, St. Louis, and elsewhere, in public schools and in private Catholic or Lutheran ("parochial") schools, to the discomfort of nativists and those concerned with the assimilation of immigrants. In 1889, the historian David Tyack tells us, Illinois and Wisconsin "tried to regulate immigrant private and parochial schools by requiring that most instruction be conducted in English. As in the case of Protestant rituals in the schools, the contest over instruction in languages other than English became a symbolic battle between those who wanted to impose one standard of belief and those who welcomed pluralistic forms of education."[2]

The First World War, with its encouragement of a fierce national (or was it ethnic?) chauvinism, finished off German as a language of instruction in public schools, and for a while even curtailed the teaching of German as a foreign language. But it was during the build-up to entry into the war, and in response to the attacks on "hyphenated Americans" by Woodrow Wilson and Theodore Roosevelt, that the first major arguments in favor of multiculturalism in American education were set forth. "Cultural pluralism" was the term Horace Kallen, a follower of John Dewey, used to describe a new kind of polity and a new kind of public education, in which a variety of cultures besides that of England

and English-influenced America would receive a significant place in American public education. His essay, "Democracy versus the Melting-Pot," appeared in *The Nation* in 1915. Randolph Bourne, a radical young journalist of the time who had written a book on the progressive Dewey-influenced schools in Gary, Indiana, and who was admired by Van Wyck Brooks and Lewis Mumford, among others, later during the war made a similar case in *The Atlantic*, in an essay titled "Transnational America."[3]

Dewey himself, in 1916, speaking to the National Education Association, took up the cudgels for cultural pluralism. He criticized the attacks on "hyphenated Americanism" that had been directed primarily against German Americans and Irish Americans for their resistance to supporting England in the war against Germany:

> Such terms as Irish-American or Hebrew-American or German-American are false terms, because they seem to assume something which is already in existence called America, to which the other factors may be hitched on. The fact is, the genuine American, the typical American, is himself a hyphenated character. It does not mean that he is part American and that some foreign ingredient is then added. It means that . . . he is international and interracial in his make-up. He is not American plus Pole or German. But the American is himself Pole-German-English-French-Spanish-Italian-Greek-Irish-Scandinavian-Bohemian-Jew—and so on. The point is to see to it that the hyphen connects instead of separates. And this means at least that our public schools shall teach each factor to respect every other, and shall take pains to enlighten us all as to the great past contributions of every strain in our composite make-up.[4]

So spoke the exemplary American philosopher from Burlington, Vermont. (One may note the complete absence of any reference to Negroes, as they were then called, in these early pleas for cultural pluralism.) But if Dewey, Kallen, and Bourne play a role in the history of multiculturalism, it is only as advocates without any direct influence on schools. The wave of post–World War I chauvinism which led to the deportation of many East Europeans as alien radicals to Bolshevist Russia, to the banning of mass immigration in 1924, to the rise of the Ku Klux Klan, was too strong to allow the proposals of a Kallen, a Bourne, or a Dewey to have much effect. Nebraska banned the teaching of any foreign language before the eighth grade (the Nebraska law exempted Greek, Latin, and Hebrew, all presumed safely dead). Oregon banned private schools altogether. Both laws were overturned by the Supreme Court.[5] In the public schools, Americanization was the order of the day and prevailed without a check through the 1920s, '30s, and '40s, while the children of the last great wave of European immigration were being educated.

I attended the schools of New York City from 1929 to 1944 (I include the public City College of New York in that stretch), and not a whiff of cultural pluralism was to be found. The public schools of New York City were then two-thirds or more Jewish and Italian in student composition, but no Jewish figure was to be found in our texts for reading or writing, for literature, for social studies, for history. And while we learned about Columbus in elementary school, and Mazzini and Garibaldi made an appearance in high school European history, there was no implication that they had any connection with our Italian fellow-students. Garibaldi and Mazzini were part of the European history text on the rise of nationalism and the unification of Germany and Italy. They were neither intended nor expected to contribute to the self-esteem of Italian American schoolchildren, and one doubts that they did. For Jewish students, the curriculum and the texts were a complete blank.

This background, which most of my generation has experienced, of a strong, unself-conscious, self-confident Americanization, in which all cultures but that of the founding English and its American variant were ignored, and in which students were left to assume that the cultures of their homes and parental homelands were inferior, is crucial in the current debates over multiculturalism. The conflict that led to the creation of the Catholic parochial school system, the abolition of German-language public schools, and the arguments for multiculturalism in the age of mass immigration are all a kind of murky prehistory, wiped out in a flood of Americanization that deposited a uniform silt over our past, leaving only fossil remains of that earlier diversity. Advocates of a multiculturalist curriculum often do not know they had forebears, while opponents often do not realize that the education they experienced was the expression of an age singularly free of conflict over issues of cultural pluralism or multiculturalism.

The arguments for cultural pluralism began to emerge again in World War II, and the motivating force was Hitler. He proclaimed that one race, one people, was superior and should be dominant, he spread hatred of Jews and Negroes, and we were at war with him, so it was in the interest of the war effort to teach the opposite: All peoples were equal, and tolerance must be extended to all. During and after the war, a modest movement for "intercultural education" sprouted: Its aim was to teach something about the various ethnic and racial groups that made up America, and to teach tolerance. Just how extensive it actually was in the schools is not clear, but it did not survive the 1950s — neither the word nor the movement.[6]

The issues of the 1950s and '60s pushed cultural pluralism aside. All eyes and all energy were focused on the desegregation of schools: the overcoming of legal segregation in the South and de facto segregation in the North. There was something of a contradiction between desegregation, as then envisaged, and cultural pluralism. The aim of black and liberal civil rights leaders was to provide the *same* education for all. Blacks would now get the education that whites had previously received. *Their* education had precious little of cultural pluralism or multiculturalism in it. Why should that be changed for blacks? The black objective, through the entire course of the struggle for equality in the courts in the 1940s, '50s, and '60s, was assimilation: Blacks should not be treated differently from whites merely because they were black.

In the later 1960s that central dogma was transmuted very rapidly into the demand of many militants that blacks must get something different *because* they were black. By the late 1960s the Black Power movement, the rise of black Muslims, and other manifestations of black nationalism were already challenging the assimilationist civil rights leadership. All-black schools were established in many black communities, and some were even established under the aegis of liberal public school systems (as in Berkeley, California).

Meanwhile, Mexican Americans and Puerto Ricans raised their own grievances against a public school system that had taught them in English and had in some places banned even the speaking of Spanish. Civil rights laws that guaranteed equality were interpreted by the Supreme Court to mean that equality for those speaking a foreign language could require instruction in that language. Liberal states passed laws giving a limited right to instruction in one's native language, and federal laws and regulations and court decisions made that a requirement in many school systems.

Bilingual education is of course not the same thing as multiculturalism, but the reality of bilingual teaching, which meant in fact the teaching of school subjects for some time in the home language of students and by teachers native in that language, had substantial consequences for *what* was taught. Bilingual instruction for students speaking Spanish also meant to some degree instruction in Puerto Rican or Mexican culture and history. Visiting schools in New York in the 1980s, I could see maps of Puerto Rico facing maps of the United States, both of the same size — they are after all the same shape, more or less — and posters of Puerto Rican heroes

▲ ▲ ▲

on the walls. Language, it was clear, was the medium of instruction for a distinctive curriculum. Through the 1970s, bilingual education and the acknowledgment of distinctive group cultures and histories in social studies and history spread and established themselves in the public schools.

The issues of multiculturalism in the 1970s and '80s no longer dealt much with European immigrants or ethnic groups. European mass immigration never recovered, even after immigration reform in 1965. Immigration became overwhelmingly Asian, Latin American, and Caribbean. Assimilation had radically transformed the children and grandchildren of European immigrants. If a few voices were raised in the 1970s from representatives of these groups claiming "Us, too!" there was very little response, and quite properly, from the public schools. One can find Russian and Italian bilingual classes in New York, and Massachusetts schools provide some transitional education in Portuguese in Fall River, Armenian in Watertown. But these are clearly understood to be temporary adaptations. No one expects that full-scale bilingual and bicultural programs for European or Asian groups will be established. The issue of multiculturalism today affects primarily the Spanish-speaking groups from Latin America and the Caribbean, whose numbers have grown hugely in the 1970s and '80s. But above all it affects blacks, America's permanent dilemma.

One might well ask, why did multiculturalism become a great issue in the schools only in the late 1980s? It is after all at least twenty-five years since public schools started adapting themselves to the presumed cultural distinctiveness and interests of two major groups in the public schools, blacks and Hispanics, by modifying textbooks, introducing new reading materials, changing examinations, instructing non-English-speaking students in Spanish for a few years. What happened to put the issue on the agenda in the late 1980s, not only in the public schools but in colleges and universities, public and private?

There is no way of giving a determinative answer to such a question; many factors can be referred to. But I believe the basic explanation is that in the late 1980s there was a build-up of frustration in the black population over the failure of civil rights reforms to deliver what was expected from them. In the colleges, affirmative action, well-established as it was, had not increased markedly the number of black instructors, or the number of black students who could qualify for the more selective institutions without special consideration. In the public schools, we had seen some modest improvement in black achievement as measured by NAEP (National Assessment of Educational Progress) scores, SAT scores, high school completion rates. But the gaps between black and white achievement remained very large. Blacks on the whole did worse than Hispanics, though one might have expected the achievement of Hispanics to be hobbled, in comparison with that of blacks, by the very large numbers of non-English-speaking Hispanic immigrants of recent years. Blacks scored far below the various Asian groups, though among the latter one would have reason to expect language difficulties to hamper their educational advance. One can record a substantial measure of black achievement in politics, in the armed forces, in the civil service, in the gaining of some high positions in the private economy, but these successes were accompanied by a host of social problems afflicting a large part of the black population, problems which by some key measures have grown, not declined, in the past twenty years.

Was the multicultural debate fueled by the large new immigration of the past twenty-five years (though not by any means as large as the immigration of the first two decades of this century)? Immigrants have been the subjects, not the protagonists, in the battles over multiculturalism; they were not the moving force. Asians, who make up almost half the number of new immigrants, seem quite content with the education they get. And they do very well, on standardized tests and on entry into selective colleges, with the

education they get, devoid as it is, for the most part, of any reference to themselves, their communities, their homelands, their culture. If there are demands for more Asian recognition or Asian
content in the curriculum, they more likely come from assimilated
and native-born militants, not from immigrants and their representatives.

What has agitated Asian Americans is not the absence of their
native cultures and languages from school curricula but rather the
discrimination they experienced in the 1980s in admission to selective colleges and universities. They seem perfectly content with a
Eurocentric curriculum. Science and mathematics, to which Asians
are often drawn as offering the best opportunity to display their
assiduity and talents and the best access to good jobs, are the same
in all languages.

Hispanics consist of at least four major groups, each with somewhat different interests and orientations. Mexican Americans, the
largest, consist of two elements: those who have been settled in the
United States for some time, some for centuries, and large numbers
of new immigrants. In time the immigrants learn English and lose
interest in Mexico. Although it is premature to say that their development will be similar to that of older European immigrant groups,
this is not an unlikely prospect. Their assimilation is affected by the
still continuing massive immigration from Mexico, by their physical
closeness to Mexico, by the prevailing atmosphere of grievance that
the media and militant leaders encourage for all "minority groups,"
and indeed by the legal establishment of rights to bilingual education and to Spanish-language assistance in voting. All these factors
will slow their assimilation. Yet I do not think their demands on the
public school system mean any necessary radical change.

Mexican Americans would like to see their children do better in
school, to have more of them graduate, and it is not clear how
strong their conviction is that this objective will be enhanced by
more teaching in Spanish, more Mexican cultural and historical

content. Activists call for this, but if their demands resonate in the Mexican American community, it is likely this is because ordinary Mexican Americans interpret the reduction of teaching in Spanish as indicating a lack of respect for and hostility to Mexican immigrants, rather than because they strongly believe it should be the function of the school to teach their children in Spanish. If the Mexican Americans do not do as well in education as they wish, the most obvious explanations are their class position as immigrants with lower levels of education, and the predominance of new immigrants. Both will change over time.

Puerto Ricans, concentrated in New York, do worse economically and perhaps educationally than Mexican Americans. One reason for that is the frequent movement back and forth between Puerto Rico and the mainland. As citizens of the United States, Puerto Ricans are not required to make a break from their homeland or to make the commitment to a new land and language that immigrants must. Puerto Rican leaders do call for more bilingual education, more Puerto Rican content, but their level of militancy does not approach that of black advocates.

Cubans now dominate Miami and Dade County, politically and educationally; they can do there what they want. And what they want seems to be a sound education with a large admixture of culturally distinctive content. Other Latin Americans, from the Dominican Republic, Central America, Colombia—in New York City they are now as numerous as Puerto Ricans—seem very much like earlier immigrants: They want to get ahead through the schools, and they see no special need to transform the schools culturally. Indeed, Central and South Americans are often to be found among those who contest the bilingual education requirements that lead school authorities to place their children in Spanish-language classes.

Native Americans, by far the smallest of the minority groups, have many special schools and colleges located on reservations.

They make up increasing numbers in some cities. As the indigenous inhabitants of the continent, they are in a very different position from immigrant groups, Hispanics, and blacks, and have a variety of special legal rights. They are also distinctive in that there is no way of telling the American story without telling *their* story, and giving them a substantial place in American literature and history. American ideology never included the hope or expectation that American Indians would, like immigrants or blacks, become part of the "melting pot," the American mainstream, though that is in fact what is happening. Even those of us educated long before multiculturalism was thought of will recall being taught about moccasins, canoes, tepees, and other aspects of American Indian culture (as it was then called) and about the adaptation of these peoples to the natural environment. Native Americans today demand more, and we now tell a larger part of their story and feel more badly about how they were treated. But the demands of Native American activists pose no challenge to any major tenet of American ideology and can be accommodated with little strain on the values of the traditional curriculum. Furthermore, Native Americans make up less than one percent of the population, and owing to high rates of intermarriage, even that number is dwindling. (Indeed, depending on how we count native Americans in the census, they may make up considerably less than one percent.)

Blacks are the storm troops in the battles over multiculturalism. They are by far the largest group involved, they feel the issues most urgently, their problems are the most severe, and their claim that they must play a larger role in the teaching of American literature and history, indeed should serve to reshape these subjects, has a far greater authority and weight than that of any other group. The most extreme version of this view, Afrocentrism, has become perhaps the most alarming aspect of the whole situation to those who are skeptical about multicultural education. And just as the black pride and black separatist movements of the late 1960s and early

1970s led to echoes and imitation among other groups, so does the present movement.

I do not question the motives of Native American, Hispanic, and Asian educators who call for more in the curriculum about their cultures. But we would not be seeing the present uproar over multiculturalism were it not for the frustration among blacks over widespread educational failure among their youth, which leads them to cast about for alternatives, new departures, new approaches, anything that might help, whether vouchers for private schools in Milwaukee, or special schools for black boys in Detroit, or Afrocentric education.

What happened to make blacks the storm troops of multiculturalism? Why have so many blacks moved against assimilation as an ideal, one that black leaders from Frederick Douglass to Martin Luther King, Jr., once adhered to with a full commitment? The answer, I am convinced, is to be found in black experience in America, and in the fundamental refusal of other Americans to accept blacks, despite their eagerness, as suitable candidates for assimilation. One result of this refusal has been to undermine assimilation as an ideal for all Americans.

6 ▲▲▲▲▲▲▲▲▲▲▲▲▲▲▲▲▲▲

WHERE ASSIMILATION FAILED

Assimilation is not today a popular term. Recently I asked a group of Harvard students taking a class on race and ethnicity in the United States what their attitude was to the term "assimilation." The large majority had a negative reaction to it. Had I asked what they thought of the term "Americanization," the reaction I am sure would have been even more hostile. The "melting pot" is no longer a uniformly praised metaphor for American society, as it once was. It suggests too much a forced conformity and reminds people today not of the welcome in American society to so many groups and races but rather of American society's demands on those it allows to enter. Indeed, in recent years it has been taken for granted that assimilation — as an expectation of how different ethnic and racial groups would respond to their common presence in one society, or as an ideal of how the society should evolve, or as the expected result of a sober social scientific analysis of the ultimate consequence of the meeting of people and races — is to be rejected. Our ethnic and racial reality, we are told, does not exhibit the effects of assimilation; our social science should not expect it; and as an ideal it has become somewhat disreputable,

96

opposed to the reality of both individual and group difference and to the claims that such differences should be recognized and celebrated.

One might think there is nothing left to say. The idea that it would happen, that it should happen, has simply been discredited, and we live with a new reality. This new reality was once called cultural pluralism; it is now called multiculturalism. And whatever the complications created by the term for educational policy, or for public policy in various other realms, that is what we must live with, and all of us seem to be ranged along a spectrum of greater or lesser enthusiasm for and acceptance of the new reality. Even critics of multiculturalism take their place within this spectrum. Those who truly stand against it, the true advocates and prophets of full assimilationism, are so minuscule in American public and intellectual life that they can scarcely be discerned in public discussion. One can point to the journal *Chronicles,* and scarcely anything else. Neither liberals nor neoliberals, conservatives nor neoconservatives, have much good to say about assimilation, and only a branch of paleoconservatism can now be mustered in its defense; its adherents would argue that even if assimilation has not yet happened, it is something which, despite the reverses of the past thirty years, should have happened, and should still happen.

Yet assimilation, properly understood, is neither a dead hope nor a demeaning concept. It is rather, I will argue, still the most powerful force affecting the ethnic and racial elements of the United States. Our problem in recognizing this has to do with the one great failure of assimilation in American life, the incorporation of African Americans—a failure that has led, in its turn, to a more general counterattack on the ideology of assimilation.

But to go back: What was assimilation? It was the expectation that a new man would be born, was being born, in the United States. We can go back to that much-quoted comment on what was the American, in Crèvecoeur's *Letters from an American Farmer* of

1782: "What then is the American, this new man? He is either a European or the descendant of a European, hence that strange mixture of blood, which you will find in no other country. I could point out to you a family whose grandfather was an Englishman, whose wife was Dutch, whose son married a French woman, and whose present four sons have four wives of four different nations. *He* is an American, who, leaving behind him all his ancient prejudices and manners, receives new ones from the new mode of life he has embraced, the new government he obeys, and the new rank he holds."[1]

This passage, which Philip Gleason tells us "has probably been quoted more than any other in the history of immigration," has of course been generally cited to celebrate American diversity and the general acceptance of this diversity as forming the basis of a new nation, a new national identity. But in 1996 we will look at it with more critical eyes, and note what it does not include as well as what it does: There is no reference to Negroes or blacks, who then made up a fifth of the American population, or to American Indians, who were then still a vivid and meaningful, on occasion menacing, presence in the colonies. In the course of an examination of the idea of assimilation in American history, we will find many other passages which to our contemporary eyes will express a similarly surprising unconsciousness, or hypocrisy, or unawareness. Today we would cry out, "There were others you are not talking about! What about them, and what place will they have in the making of the new American?"

The concept of assimilation looked toward Europe. It referred to the expected experience and fate of the stream of immigrants who were a permanent part of American life and consciousness from the time of the first settlements on the Atlantic seaboard to the 1920s, when it was thought (incorrectly) that we were now done with mass immigration of people of varied backgrounds to the United States.

There has been a good deal of discussion of the significance of one major characteristic of the emerging American national consciousness, or, we would say today, the emerging American identity: In many authoritative formulations, from the Declaration of Independence on, the American, the new nationality being formed here, is not defined ethnically, as deriving from an ancient common stock or stocks, as almost all other major modern nations define themselves. I may point out as an aside that while the term "identity" is almost essential in any discussion of this emerging American national character, it is a relative latecomer to the discussion. Philip Gleason tells us:

> The term "identity" has become indispensable in the discussion of ethnic affairs. Yet it was hardly used at all until the 1950s. The father of the concept, Erik H. Erikson, remarked on its novelty in . . . *Childhood and Society* (1950): "We begin to conceptualize matters of identity . . . in a country which attempts to make a super-identity of all the identities imported by its constituent immigrants." In an autobiographical account published 20 years later, Erikson . . . quoted this passage and added that the terms "identity" and "identity crisis" seemed to grow out of "the experience of emigration, immigration, and Americanization."[2]

Many could be quoted on this surprising characteristic of American identity, and on the avoidance or very limited presence of explicit ethnic reference in the founding documents and in the debates on the Revolution and the formation of the Union. Despite the fact that the American Revolution was fought almost exclusively by men who traced their origins to the British Isles, and primarily to England, and that the signers of the Declaration of Independence and the framers of the Constitution were exclusively of this stock, they did not define their Americanness as an ethnic characteristic. They emphasized its dependence on adherence to ideals, to universal principles. Perhaps, as Gleason points out, it was because it was necessary for the rebels and revolutionaries to distinguish themselves from the ethnically almost identical country against which they were rebelling.

But in any case, the preference for an ideological formulation of the definition of the American was there at the beginning. Years ago I quoted Hans Kohn, Yehoshua Arieli, and S. M. Lipset on this characteristic of American identity.[3] One could add other voices. As Gleason writes, "The ideological quality of American national identity was of decisive importance, vis-à-vis the question of immigration and ethnicity. To become an American a person did not have to be of any particular national, linguistic, religious, or ethnic background. All he had to do was to commit himself to the political ideology centered on the abstract ideals of liberty, equality, and republicanism. Thus the universalist ideological character of American nationality meant that it was open to anyone who willed to become an American."[4] As anyone writing in 1980 must be, he is aware of the exclusions, not remarked on by the writers of those early ringing documents, perhaps exclusions of which they were not conscious, the blacks and American Indians, and later other groups not in the beginning present in the new United States. Even if they were not specifically excluded, they were not intended to be included in these ringing affirmations of universality.

One could find here and there before the 1940s a few voices of significance who seem to make no exclusion. There was Emerson in 1845: "In this continent—asylum of all nations—the energy of Irish, Germans, Swedes, Poles, and Cossacks, and all the European tribes—of the Africans, and of the Polynesians—will construct a new race, a new religion, a new state, a new literature, which will be as vigorous as the new Europe which came out of the smelting-pot of the Dark Ages."[5] There was Whitman. But one can ask even of Emerson, did he mean it? What did he know of Polynesians, after all? And one can ask of the term he introduced to characterize the assimilation of the different elements, the "smelting pot," later to achieve fame in the form of the "melting pot," was that not too brutal, too strong a metaphor for what was to be lost, to disappear, in order to make this new race? The groups were to be more than melted, smelted, as in two or more metals becoming one (the Emerson passage begins with a reference to "Corinthian brass").

If we look back toward the nineteenth century from the perspective of the present, we can only be surprised at how unconcerned Americans were over the problem of assimilation until the 1890s or so. John Higham has pointed to this oddity, but notes that this unconcern was possible only because other races simply did not enter into the consideration of the issue. As he writes:

> To speak of assimilation as a problem in nineteenth-century America is, in an important sense, to indulge in anachronism. That is because nineteenth-century Americans seemed for the most part curiously undaunted by, and generally insensitive to, the numerous and sometimes tragic divisions in their society along racial and ethnic lines . . . Assimilation was either taken for granted or viewed as inconceivable. For European peoples it was thought to be the natural, almost inevitable, outcome of life in America. For other races assimilation was believed to be largely unattainable and therefore not a source of concern. Only at the end of the century did ethnic mixing arouse a sustained and urgent sense of danger. Only then did large numbers of white Americans come to fear that assimilation was *not* occurring among major European groups and that it was going too far among other minorities, notably blacks, Orientals, and Jews.[6]

In almost all the discussions of Americanization or assimilation until about World War II, the participants have only Europeans in mind. This is true whether they favored or opposed assimilation and Americanization efforts. Today, a reader of the documents of the great Americanization drive of the second decade of this century will find no reference to blacks, then as now our largest minority. It is as if the turmoil of abolitionism, slavery, the Civil

War, Reconstruction did not exist. All concern was with the enormous numbers of "new" immigrants from Eastern and Southern Europe, who were different from the Europeans the nation had become accustomed to. Admittedly one could make the argument that "Americanization," the name of the assimilation movement of the time, could address only those who were not Americans, and that blacks, being American-born and formally citizens, did not qualify for the discussion. So, one could argue, this was the reason they were ignored in the great debate that finally degenerated into a resurgent Ku Klux Klan and the closing of the gates to the new immigrants.

Yet when one looks at the aims of the Americanization movement, one may well ask, and why not blacks too? The aims of the movement, in its earlier, benign form, were to make the newcomers citizens and encourage them to participate as individuals in politics (as against their domination by urban bosses), to teach them English (and here one main argument was to make them better and safer workers, in view of the huge toll of industrial accidents), to break up immigrant colonies ("distribution," it was called), and to teach American customs, which to the Americanizers seemed to mean primarily sanitation and hygiene. All this would make the immigrants better Americans.

One major motivation for Americanization was concern that the new immigrants, because they did not speak English, were not citizens, and had little knowledge of American customs, would not become good Americans. To this concern was added the fear of lack of patriotism or disloyalty, which peaked during World War I. The vigorous advocates of Americanization—social workers and businessmen, a strange mix that nevertheless characterized much of the progressivism of the time—were trying to plead the case of the new immigrants against those of their countrymen who increasingly favored immigration restriction. The social workers, we know, pled this case out of understanding and sympathy for the new immigrants. The businessmen, we may assume, took the same position primarily out of self-interest, much as the *Wall Street Journal* today argues for free immigration. The aim of the Americanization movement was to integrate outsiders. But if so, why were blacks not included?

Their exclusion is even more striking in view of the language of the time, in which ethnic groups are referred to as "races." But what comes to mind today when we speak of "race" are not the European groups that were the concern of the earnest and energetic advocates of assimilation and Americanization; it is blacks, African Americans. Consider one of the most authoritative statements of what was hoped for from Americanization, from a progressive woman social worker who was the heart and soul of the movement, indefatigably organizing committees, conventions, statements, programs, Frances Kellor:

> Americanization is the science of racial relations in America, dealing with the assimilation and amalgamation of diverse races in equity into an integral part of the national life. By "assimilation" is meant the indistinguishable incorporation of the races into the substance of American life. By "amalgamation" is meant so perfect a blend that the absence or imperfection of any of the vital racial elements available, will impair the compound. By "an integral part" is meant that, once fused, separation of units is thereafter impossible. By "in equity" is meant impartiality among the races accepted into the blend with no imputations of inferiority and no bestowed favors.[7]

This is a late statement, made when the movement was taking on a harsher tone, and rather stronger than we would find from most advocates of Americanization (in particular in its emphasis on "amalgamation," which can only mean intermarriage to the point of the indistinguishability of any distinct group), but the point in quoting this statement is that we may take it for granted, in the light

of the attitude toward black-white intermarriage that then prevailed, that Francis Kellor simply did not have blacks in mind,
despite the continual emphasis on the word "race."

One of the early climaxes of the movement was a great meeting
in Philadelphia, on May 10, 1915. Woodrow Wilson addressed a
huge throng: 5,000 newly naturalized citizens, 8,000 previously
naturalized, with a chorus of 5,000 voices, and the like. He does not
use the term "race" in his paean to the all-inclusiveness of America;
but all races are clearly implied in his term "the people of the
world": "This is the only country in the world which experiences
this constant and repeated rebirth. Other countries depend upon
the multiplication of their own native people. This country is constantly drinking strength out of new sources by the voluntary
association with it of great bodies of strong men and forward-look-
ing women out of other lands . . . It is as if humanity had determined to see to it that this great Nation, founded for the benefit of
humankind, should not lack for the allegiance of the people of the
world."[8] But we might again ask, where were the blacks? Clearly
Wilson did not have them in mind.

This great meeting was the prelude to Americanization Day on
July 4, 1915, when many mass meetings to welcome new citizens
were held all over the country. One of them was in Faneuil Hall in
Boston, addressed by Justice Brandeis. He asserted that what was
distinctly American is "inclusive brotherhood." America, as against
other nations, "has always declared herself for equality of nationalities as well as for equality of individuals. It recognizes racial
equality as an essential of full human liberty and true brotherhood
. . . It has, therefore, given like welcome to all the peoples of
Europe."[9] "The peoples of Europe" is what he has in mind, not
blacks.

Most ironically, we find that one of the most active of the postwar Americanization groups was the Inter-Racial Council. We
know what that term would have meant had it been used twenty

years later. But in 1919 it struck no one as odd, apparently, that it did not refer to blacks at all and it did not include blacks. Among a host of names of leading businessmen and bankers and political dignitaries we find some prominent immigrant names (Dr. Antonio Stella, M. I. Pupin, Gutzon Borglum, Jacob Schiff) but no blacks.[10]

The Americanization movement began to shift from one befriending the immigrant, bringing him closer to other Americans, to one which seemed increasingly hostile, in which the generous offer of citizenship and full participation became the compulsory demand that the immigrant must learn English and American government. In response to this development, the Carnegie Corporation, trying to defend the earlier openness toward the immigrant, the spirit expressed by Jane Addams and Lillian Wald, sponsored a series of "Americanization Studies." Once again the language in these studies will surprise us in its unconsciousness of the fact that "race" might include other than Europeans.

In James A. Gavit's book *Americans by Choice,* on the issue of naturalization, we find again the argument with which we are familiar: The American is not defined ethnically; he is defined by allegiance to an ideology. "The American Has No Racial Marks," one subtitle asserts. Gavit goes on to say:

> This absence of exclusive racial marks is the distinguishing physical characteristic of the American. True of him as of no other now or ever in the past is the fact that he is, broadly speaking, the product of *all* races . . . We are in the midst of the making of the "American." He does not yet appear what he shall be but one thing is certain, he is not to be of any particular racial type now distinguishable. Saxon, Teuton, Kelt, Latin and Slav— to say nothing of any appreciable contribution by yellow and brown races as yet negligible . . . —each of the races that we now know on this soil will have its share of "ancestorial" responsibility for the "typical American" that is to be.[11]

The next heading reads, "Not Racial, But Cultural." Dealing as he does with naturalization, Gavit cannot, as more celebratory advocates of Americanization can, totally ignore the racial aspect: Naturalization was then racially limited. Only whites (and Africans!) could become citizens. He does write: "It is not yet true — perhaps it will be very long before it can be true — that there is absolutely no bar to any person on account of race; for the law and its interpretations exclude from citizenship Chinese, Japanese, and certain people of India not regarded as 'white' — although the blacks of Africa are expressly admitted. Nevertheless, it may be said broadly that regardless of race, the immigrant can come to America and win his way upon his own merits into the fellowship all the world calls 'Americans.'"[12] There is no comment on the fact that despite their formal equality as citizens, blacks were not allowed to participate in politics in the South.

We will find a similar liberal and welcoming tone in another volume of the Carnegie Corporation's Americanization series, *The Schooling of the Immigrant*, by Frank V. Thompson, then superintendent of Boston's public schools. It is mostly concerned with the teaching of English and of American ideals and habits, which are left rather unspecified and vague. The students he has in mind in most of the book are adults who he hopes will become naturalized. When it comes to schoolchildren, the children of immigrants, nothing much is proposed. The author has confidence in the assimilatory powers of the American public school, and while he commends some contemporary distinctive programs for immigrant children (not sufficiently specified to give any clear impression of what they do), he feels Americanization requires little in the way of special adaptation, and what little is required is the teaching of how American government works.

He writes: "An astonishing fact about the work of the common school is that Americanization has scarcely been a conscious motive. Americanization has taken place through the schools but it has been an unconscious by-product . . . specifically the teacher has been concerned with the fundamental processes of education and with the fine and industrial arts." He thinks more attention should be paid specifically to "training in citizenship," and notes that teachers receive a good deal of training, and fulfill various requirements for promotion, "but nowhere among these is there a test of acquainticeship with the problem of Americanization."[13]

So as regards schoolchildren he expresses no great concern: Despite the lack of specific attention, "Americanization and citizenship are usual resultants of all school training. The child receives impressions, inspirations, and impulses from the pictures he sees in the classroom, from the stories he reads in his history, from the exercises he attends in the assembly hall, from the celebration of patriotic anniversaries and the salute of the flag. We furnish special classes sometimes for non-English-speaking children, but we do so merely for the purpose of enabling these children to enter the regular grades without delay."[14]

All this is very far from what we later came to know as intercultural education, which emphasized education in tolerance, and even further from the present varieties of multiculturalism. There is supreme confidence in the assimilatory powers of American society and its distinctive agent, the public school. No special programs are required aside from the teaching of English and the strengthening of the rather puerile civics courses of the day. Thompson pays no attention to the distinctive culture of European children of different ethnic groups or religions. He does consider whether *any* distinctive variation for immigrant children in the public education generally provided is necessary, and he is doubtful. As he writes: "It is to our credit that in our schools we have never made invidious comparisons with respect to the children of the immigrant; we have received them on a basis of equality and made them feel that there were no distinctions on account of accidents of birth and circumstance."[15]

Nevertheless he does recommend that just as we make special provision for various kinds of "atypical" children, there should be some special provision to take account of the fact that "the majority of immigrant children, while normal with respect to range of mental capacities, do differ in social and economic condition from the children of families settled here for generations. The immigrant child . . . frequently suffers from the handicap of a foreign language in the household, and often from the inexperience of his parents in the American environment." What he seems to have in mind is the "steamer classes," common then for newly arrived immigrant children in some large cities. These did not usually last for more than a few months.[16]

We see here the characteristic assumption of the period that the assimilation of European children is no very difficult matter, and the characteristic silence in regard to black children. Nor is there any reference to Asian children, and yet the question of separate schools for Japanese-American children had been and was an issue in California. Even when Thompson has a section titled "The South Awakened to Illiteracy," his main point is that there are few immigrants in the Deep South, and the problem there is rather the substantial degree of illiteracy among the native population. He may have had blacks as well as whites in mind, though there is no reference to blacks. What centrally concerned him was to encourage tolerance and welcome, and appropriate kinds of assistance, for the European immigrant, adult or child.

As we know, the Americanization movement lost its aspect of welcome and inclusion in the midst of the passions aroused by World War I and the postwar fear of Bolshevism and radicalism. It turned into something harsh and oppressive, in which the issue became less the opportunity to learn English than the insistence that nothing but English be learned; less the generous offer of citizenship than the widespread fear of subversion from aliens and naturalized citizens. Americanization developed a bad name among

liberals. Insofar as there was still concern for the living and working conditions of immigrants, this became encompassed in a larger
liberal movement for improving the conditions of working men and
women generally, a movement that was easily capable of reconcil-
ing commitment to the cause of working people with opposition to
further immigration. If the word "assimilation" now makes us suspicious, and "Americanization" even more so, it is in part because
of the excesses of the 1920s.

The term "Americanization" is no longer to be found in encyclo-
pedias of the social sciences,[17] but it does appear in the first great
Encyclopedia of the Social Sciences of 1930, and the comment we find
there on the fate of Americanization will to some extent explain to
us why we do not hear much about it today:

> This emphasis on the learning of English and naturalization,
> together with the unfortunate atmosphere of coercion and con-
> descension in which so many wartime Americanization efforts
> were conceived, had the effect of bringing the word into a disre-
> pute from which it has never fully recovered. Contributing to the
> same result, in the period following the war, were the widely
> expressed fear and suspicion of the immigrant, his frequent in-
> dictment as a radical, attempts to suppress his newspapers and
> organizations, the ignoring of his own culture and aspirations,
> the charge that certain nationalities and races were inferior and
> unassimilable, and the use of intimidating slogans. Americaniza-
> tion work too frequently made the assumption that American
> culture was something already complete which the newcomer
> must adopt in its entirety. Such attitudes and activities were
> important factors in promoting restriction of immigration, but
> they did not advance the assimilation of the immigrants who were
> already in America.[18]

My point in reciting episodes in the history of Americanization
is not to add to the extensive literature that explores the neglect of
the key question of the treatment of blacks in American society; nor

to argue, which is true, that immigrants were better treated and taken more seriously than blacks from the point of view of their inclusion in American society; nor to attack the Americanization movement for its excesses—all legitimate responses to it. It is to set the stage for something that has also received little attention: that the *critics* of Americanization and assimilation also had nothing or little to say about blacks. However passionate their defense of the contribution to American economy, culture, and politics of immigrants and immigrant groups, however strong their resistance to the demand for assimilation, whatever the arguments they raised against the value of assimilation, the critics of Americanization and assimilation—we can call them for convenience the "cultural pluralists"—had little to say, indeed nothing to say, about adding blacks to the groups who they felt had every right to maintain their separate identity. Maybe they believed blacks should preserve their separate identity, maybe they never thought about the matter. Blacks just never entered into the argument.

There were critics of Americanization, fewer in its earlier more benign form, more when it evolved under the pressures of war into an attack on "hyphenated Americans," even more when it further evolved into the repression of the postwar years. Thus Americanization became associated with laws restricting immigration, limiting the rights of aliens, banning teaching in foreign languages (and on occasion even teaching foreign languages), and with harsh administrative actions expelling aliens. A powerful wave of nativist public opinion led to the sharp restriction of further immigration from Europe, and the nation experienced the mass hysteria of the Ku Klux Klan and similar organizations. But it is interesting to note that the few voices raised in criticism of extreme Americanization and in defense of cultural pluralism—voices that in recent decades we have disinterred—had almost nothing to say about blacks. This was true of Randolph Bourne in his advocacy of "Transnational America." It was true of Horace Kallen in his insistence that each group, each "race," in the language of the time, had an inherent genius or character that should not be suppressed but allowed to flower. We search this modest literature in vain for any reference to black Americans.[19]

Thus, when John Dewey spoke to the National Education Association in 1916 to defend the value of cultural pluralism, he did not seem to have blacks in mind. Of course, he was speaking in the context of an attack on the loyalty of European Americans, in the language of the time, "hyphenated Americans." Nevertheless, one would have thought America's largest minority might have entered into the discussion. Many groups were mentioned in his talk. But no mention of blacks.[20]

One searches Kallen's *Culture and Democracy in the United States*, the fullest statement of the cultural pluralist view of the time, for any reference to blacks. They cannot be fully escaped. After all, the introductory chapter is titled "Culture and the Ku Klux Klan," and Negroes are listed as among its targets. There are two other slightly fuller references. In speaking of the spirit of Know-Nothingism, he writes: "What differs from ourselves we spontaneously set upon a different level of value. If it seems to be strong it is called wicked and is feared; if it is regarded as weak, it is called brutish and exploited. Sometimes, as in the attitude toward the negro [sic], the emotions interpenetrate and become a sentiment focalizing the worst qualities of each." There is one more reference. He is concerned in this passage with whether the current hysteria will wane, the integration of immigrants into American life under a liberal regime will continue (here "integration" clearly does not mean "assimilation"). But it may not happen. The immigrant may be fixed in the inferior economic position he now holds: "One need only cast an eye over the negro-white relations in the South to realize the limit that such a condition would, unchecked, engender."[21] Perhaps it is reading too much into very little, but one detects in this passage no expectation that there will be much change in the condition of the Negro.

The significance of this episode in the history of American thinking about race and ethnicity is that the argument over assimilation and Americanization evoked by the mass immigration of the period 1880–1924 and by the pressures of World War I simply did not take blacks, let alone Mexican Americans or Asians, into account.

When the issue of the relation of the immigrant and immigrant groups to American society emerged again in the late 1930s matters were very different. Now the initiating historical circumstance was the rise of Hitler, his racism and his threat to world peace. In World War I the objective of American leaders who favored the allied powers was to have the immigrant forget the country he came from. Memory and allegiance to one's past country among our largest immigrant groups (Germans, Irish) would not lead to sympathy for the Western Allies but quite the reverse. If immigrants thought of themselves only as Americans, they would more likely accept alliance with England, the country that was the enemy of their homelands. In the run-up to our entry into World War II, matters were somewhat different. Although patriotism and Americanism were hardly slighted, it generally served the interests of our national leaders that immigrant groups should remember their pasts and their homelands: So many of them were suffering under Nazi oppression.

But the opposition to Hitler involved considerably more than the strategy of using ethnic background to mobilize Americans against a foreign enemy. Hitler was an ideologist as well as a German nationalist, and his ideology was racism and anti-Semitism. Race now meant—in large measure because of Hitler and his racism— what we today understand as race, physical difference. If we were to fight racism, of course blacks could not be ignored. Mobilization in World War I meant a forceful assimilation and Americanization. Mobilization in World War II meant accentuating our tolerance, our diversity, against the racism and intolerance of Hitler. I do not mean to suggest that it was only the logic involved in the fight

against Hitler that made it impossible to ignore blacks in consider-
ing the relationship of groups of different ethnic and racial background to American society. There were many other changes that
had taken place in the America of the New Deal and Franklin D.
Roosevelt that brought blacks and their plight to public attention
more sharply than in the America of Theodore Roosevelt and
Woodrow Wilson. But certainly one factor was that American political and educational leaders wanted to emphasize our tolerance
and inclusiveness against Hitler's intolerance and exclusiveness.

Thus as something like "cultural pluralism" began to raise its
head again with the coming of Hitler and the fear of a future war,
the growing concern was no longer with European immigrants
alone, as it was in the build-up to World War I. Americans generally were not much concerned with the loyalty of German Americans or Italian Americans. Security agencies were worried about
German American adherents of Nazism, Italian adherents of Italian Fascism (much fewer), and all Japanese Americans, who were
the only group to be affected by a World War I–style popular
hysteria. So there was a reprise to some extent of World War I
concern with immigrant loyalty. Indeed, we even had a revival of
something like the Americanization Day spectacles of the earlier
period in the creation and brief history of "I Am an American
Day." But the tone of the new movement was different in some key
respects.

First, mass immigration had come to an end, and no one expected it to revive, whatever the needs of persecuted Jews and
other groups harried by the Nazis. European immigrant groups
were already well on the way to assimilation. There was no particular need for a movement to emphasize the learning of English, or
to speed naturalization. Perhaps this explains the rather benign
patriotism of World War II as compared with World War I.

But second, blacks, Hispanics, and Asians were now definitely
part of the story. Because we were fighting Hitler and his ideology

of racial superiority, we had to take into account our own groups of racially defined second-class citizens, all suffering under a weight of legal as well as informal segregation, discrimination, and prejudice. Cultural pluralism, which had been in World War I and its aftermath only the evanescent hope of a few philosophers and journalists, became a sturdy growth, under a new name, intercultural education. The focus of concern began to shift from European immigrant groups to nonwhite minorities. And in fighting the ideology of race — physical race, biological race — how could we not be concerned with how we treated our racial minorities?

What was to be the fate of assimilation in this new dispensation? Whatever the new degree of tolerance for diversity, it was generally expected that assimilation would continue. Intercultural education, which in the 1940s taught tolerance of other groups in the schools, was a far cry from a full-bodied cultural pluralism and presented no resistance to assimilation. It stood for tolerance, not for the maintenance of cultural difference and identity. Indeed, even if the term was not used, assimilation was what the advocates for our largest and most oppressed minority also wanted.[22]

The term "assimilation" was a key concept in the thinking of our most important sociologist of race and ethnicity, Robert E. Park, who established at the University of Chicago a strong commitment to the study of questions of race and ethnicity. Park and his colleagues, who had participated in the Carnegie Americanization studies after World War I, were opponents of forceful Americanization, but they nevertheless believed social trends were bringing an inevitable assimilation. They did not decry this: This was the inevitable result in time of the meeting of peoples. Park saw that the great problem checking a uniform and successful assimilation was white attitudes toward blacks.

His 1930 article on assimilation in the *Encyclopedia of the Social Sciences* perceptively points to this as the stumbling block in the way of assimilation: "In a vast, varied and cosmopolitan society such as

▲ ▲ ▲

exists in America, the chief obstacle to assimilation seems to be not cultural differences but physical traits . . . The Negro, during his three hundred years in this country, has not been assimilated. This is not because he has preserved in America a foreign culture and alien tradition . . . No man is so entirely native to the soil . . . To say the Negro is not assimilated means no more than to say that he is still regarded in some sense a stranger, a representative of an alien race . . . This distinction which sets him apart from the rest of the population is real, but is not based upon cultural traits but upon physical and racial characteristics." As for Europeans: "The ease and rapidity with which aliens have been able to take over American customs and manners have enabled the United States to digest every sort of normal human difference, with the exception of the purely external ones like that of the color of the skin."[23]

Park saw the key problem for assimilation: It was race. Black intellectuals and leaders were of course also aware that assimilation, as process or ideal, was leaving them out. They were not even participants in the debate over assimilation and Americanization. Nevertheless, in striving for the rights that would make them equal to white Americans, in aiming at a condition in which no distinction would be made between white and black Americans, they in effect were lined up with those who wanted to assimilate or integrate the immigrant. They saw no good reason for the maintenance of group distinctiveness in America. What Americanizers considered ideal for immigrants was what blacks considered as ideal for themselves. Black leaders were not asking to be part of that orchestra of difference that Horace Kallen envisaged as the ideal for America. (In fact, black culture was sturdily established and maintained its distinctiveness with no widespread intentional effort to do so, but this came naturally, so to speak, and owed nothing to the demands and hopes of black leaders.) American liberals in general, who supported black aims, also saw no good argument in principle against assimilation for all groups.

Park had set forth a scheme that became quite influential in sociology: Groups in contact moved through various phases, such as conflict and accommodation, ending in assimilation. Despite the growing attention to the plight of blacks during the 1930s and '40s, an attention encouraged by important foundation-sponsored research by white and black liberal scholars and by key legal cases, there was little challenge to the expectation that assimilation or something like it—the term "integration" became popular—was the desirable solution to the American dilemma. Certainly no liberal and no black leader favored the continuation of segregation. No significant black leader favored separatism. Marcus Garvey's Back to Africa movement was an exotic oddity, and the American Communists' temporary advocacy of a separate black state in the South an even greater oddity. Garveyism reflected more the deep frustration of the American black over his exclusion from American society than any positive commitment to the maintenance of a separate black culture. Until the late 1960s, there was no challenge to the assimilationist stance of sociologists who studied race and ethnicity and of black scholars and leaders.

Park and his leading students, while they did not put their preferences forth sharply, assumed assimilation was not only inevitable but would be all for the best. Thus, Louis Wirth, who was the chief successor to Park, made clear in his book on American Jews, *The Ghetto,* that his preference was for assimilation: The Jew continued to exist only because of prejudice and discrimination; all the reactions of the Jew to this antagonism were humanly limiting; and assimilation, which to be sure required lowering the barriers others placed in the way of assimilation, was the desirable end result of the interaction of Jews and non-Jews in contemporary society.[24]

The central work on the black condition in the United States in the 1940s, Gunnar Myrdal's *An American Dilemma,* could also be described as assimilationist.[25] This book expressed not only Myrdal's views but to some degree those of his black collaborators, major black scholars and intellectuals of the times, a number of whom were Marxists (Myrdal was not). In their view, racial and ethnic differences would in time be overcome by the development of class consciousness, bringing together blacks and whites on the basis of class interest.[26]

The major works of E. Franklin Frazier on the black family could also be described as assimilationist. Insofar as the black family was stable and puritanical it was good—that was unquestioned. There was no hint that it was desirable that any distinctive cultural feature should survive as specifically Negro or black, or that there should be any effort to seek such features.

The best-informed, most liberal, and most sympathetic analysts of the ethnic and racial scene in the 1930s and '40s saw assimilation as a desirable consequence of the reduction of prejudice and discrimination. Blacks wanted to live under circumstances no different from those whites lived under, and under these circumstances they would not be different from other Americans. It was rare to find among black intellectuals and political leaders any notion that some distinctive black culture or social practices must be protected and retained. In the face of the overwhelming task of dealing with white prejudice and discrimination, the issue of a distinctive black culture could not take a high place on any black agenda.

Although it was clear that blacks could not, because of race, be indistinguishable from whites, it was desirable that they become culturally, socially, economically, and politically assimilated, that they be simply Americans with dark skins. Until the 1960s scarcely any black leader or intellectual diverged from this view. Their demand was that all public bodies, agencies of government, schools and colleges, all private agencies that affected individual circumstances, including banks, businesses, housing producers, and landlords, be color-blind.

Among the white immigrant groups—or, to label them more properly, ethnic groups, for such they became as they maintained some degree of group cohesion and identity with the reduction in the numbers of the foreign-born — one could find the upholders of the ethnic conscience and consciousness, those who established and maintained schools, churches, philanthropic and civic organizations, insurance societies, social groups. But except among those whose direct interest was in maintaining this organizational network and the jobs it offered, these were regarded by the members of ethnic groups themselves as survivals from the age of immigration, fated to fall away as acculturation and assimilation progressed. No one was more thoroughly American than the children of immigrants, the second generation.

Acculturation and assimilation, if not the cruder "Americanization," was thus generally accepted as the way America was going and should go. This prospect was favored by old Americans, regardless of their attitudes to the newer Americans, and by the immigrants of the great migration at the end of the nineteenth and beginning of the twentieth centuries and their children. Nativists as well as liberals most sympathetic to the newer Americans accepted the inevitability and desirability of assimilation.

We are now very far from all this. The voices of opposition to assimilation burst out in the late 1960s and have gone through many permutations since. Bland intercultural education has succumbed to the rather more forceful multicultural education. That too comes in all brands, from the mildest recognition of differences to a rather hysterical and irrational Afrocentrism. We even had, in the late 1960s and '70s, a brief explosion of revived ethnic assertiveness among white European ethnic groups, the heirs of the immigrants of the early decades of the century. It could not survive; assimilation had gone too far. We have a few modest programs in Italian American studies, and a sturdier growth of Jewish programs, sturdier because Jewish programs are able to draw not only on ethnic attachments that tend to be stronger than those for most white Europeans but also on religion, which creates a robust body of institutions to parallel the purely ethnic, and which has greater prestige and receives more respect in the American setting.

We come now to our central question: Is assimilation then dead? The word may be dead, the concept may be disreputable, but the reality continues to flourish. As so many observers in the past have noted, assimilation in the United States is not dependent on public ideology, on school curricula, on public approbation. Factors in social and economic and cultural life foster it, and it proceeds apace. Read Lewis was right when, in his now more than sixty-years old article on "Americanization" in the *Encyclopedia of the Social Sciences,* he wrote: "Important as these conscious efforts are toward Americanization, they represent only a part of the social forces which play continuously upon the immigrant and determine the degree and rapidity of his assimilation. A conspicuous force which makes for adjustment is the urge to material success, which makes the immigrant adapt himself to American ways of work and business. This usually involves learning the English language as quickly as possible. Standardizing forces such as national advertisements, ten-cent store products, movies, radio and the tabloid press play also upon the immigrant."[27] Correct for inflation, add television, baseball, football, and basketball, and it is clear that the forces pressing assimilation have not lost power.

Call it "acculturation" if you will. But assimilation in its least deniable and strongest form, what was once called "amalgamation," also proceeds apace. The rates of intermarriage among all European ethnic groups are very high.[28] Even Jews, who have a strong cultural and religious bar against intermarriage and who maintained a rather low rate of intermarriage until the last two or three decades, now show very high rates (50 percent or more) of individuals marrying outside the group. With such high intermarriage rates among most ethnic groups, it will become increasingly less clear to any individual what his ethnic group is and how it is to be defined. In answer to the question, "What is this person's ancestry," asked in the Census, two-fifths of Americans give multiple ancestries.[29] Mary Waters, in *Ethnic Options*, shows how thin any sense of ethnicity among Americans of European origin has become.[30]

But there is the great exception. If intermarriage is taken as key evidence for powerful assimilatory forces, then blacks are not subject to these forces to the same degree as others. Hispanic groups and Asian groups, despite the recency of immigration of so many of them, and thus the greater power of family and group attachment, show rates of intermarriage approaching the levels of Europeans.[31] Blacks stand apart, with very low rates of intermarriage, rising slowly. They stand apart too in the degree of residential segregation.[32] Thirty years of effort, public and private, assisted by antidiscrimination law and a substantial rise in black earnings, have made little impact on this pattern.

Whatever the causes, the apartness of blacks is real. And it is this that feeds multiculturalism. For this one group, assimilation, by some key measures, has certainly failed. For other groups, multicultural education may be a matter of sentiment; but most black children do attend black majority schools, and live in black neighborhoods. Why should not multiculturalism, in the form of the examination of one's group history, characteristics, problems, become compelling as a way to understand one's situation, and perhaps overcome it? The large statements asserting that the American national ideal is inclusion and assimilation understandably will ring false to many blacks, despite the commitment of most black intellectuals and political leaders to integration.

For Hispanics and Asian Americans, marked in varying degree by race, it is in large measure a matter of choice, their choice, just how they will define their place in American society. We see elements in these groups who, in their support of bilingual education and other foreign-language rights, want to establish or preserve an institutional base for a separate identity that may maintain some

▲ ▲ ▲

resistance to the forces of assimilation. For blacks too there are choices. We see the existence of choices in the writings of black intellectuals who oppose the stronger tendencies of multiculturalism. But the difference that separates blacks from whites, and even from other groups "of color" that have undergone a history of discrimination and prejudice in this country, is not to be denied. It is this separation which is the most powerful force arguing for multiculturalism and for resistance to the assimilatory trends of American education and American society.

We have policies to deal with this apartness, in schooling, in residential location. But despite good intentions and substantial efforts, these efforts to overcome the separation of most blacks from the American mainstream have not been successful.

7

▲ ▲ ▲ ▲ ▲ ▲ ▲ ▲ ▲ ▲ ▲ ▲ ▲ ▲ ▲ ▲ ▲

CAN WE BE BROUGHT
TOGETHER?

There is nothing that concentrates the mind on an issue more sharply than discovering one has been wrong about it. Twenty years ago, in an article in *The Public Interest*,[1] I dealt with the subject of the continuing concentration of blacks in American cities, and their separation in residence from whites. The article was occasioned by Anthony Downs's book of 1973, *Opening Up the Suburbs*.[2]

The degree of concentration of blacks in cities was apparently historically unique. It was commonly referred to as "segregation," but that term was generally used until the late 1960s for state-imposed segregation. Although one could argue over the degree of state involvement in black residential concentration, in the North and West there was no substantial history of state action to separate blacks and whites. Today, that useful distinction between separation imposed by state action and separation arising from other causes, which was retained for a while in the context of school issues by the use of the two terms *de jure* and *de facto* segregation, is pretty much abandoned. Recently, the black president of the Denver school board, defending his position that busing for

122

integration, which had been in effect for twenty years, should now be abandoned, referred to its effects in increasing the number of dominantly black schools, as increasing "segregation." Concentration, whatever the cause, is now "segregation," *tout court.*

This sharp separation of whites and blacks residentially could be observed in most American cities in the 1950s and '60s and had been documented statistically in research.[3] It was already under attack in the 1960s and '70s by a variety of new federal policies, legislative, administrative, and judicial. Downs, in *Opening Up the Suburbs,* had even more extensive policies to propose. All this, I argued in my 1974 article, was unnecessary. Blacks would become residentially more integrated with whites as their economic circumstances improved, as their political power increased, and as they drew closer in all other respects to whites. And we could expect this to happen as a result of the powerful antidiscrimination legislation of 1964 and 1965.

Whatever the changes that have occurred in the black condition since that time, in this one respect—the degree of concentration of blacks in specific areas of cities and some selected suburbs, and the residential isolation of blacks in general—there has been little change in twenty years.

In many respects, alas, the commonly held expectations of the 1960s and '70s as to the future of blacks and of black-white relations have not been fulfilled. If one had been asked at the time of the passage of the Civil Rights Act in 1964 to project how matters would stand thirty years in the future, what well-informed person would have predicted the degree of separation between blacks and whites that now exists in residence, in economic conditions, in family patterns, in attitudes?

There were good reasons to believe in the mid-1970s, as I did, that the pattern of residential concentration and isolation was going to change for the better. Thus further governmental intervention— whether to strengthen the prohibition of discrimination in rental, sales, and realtor behavior, or to impose integration on new developments, or to integrate housing projects through public measures, or by action in a host of areas in which new governmental intervention was possible—was not necessary. We could have argued over whether the measures then in force proscribing discrimination in sales and rentals and segregation in government-assisted housing should be stronger, but it seemed to me in 1974 that it was now basically up to the processes of social change, abetted by the expected continuing and increased economic and social mobility of blacks, to change the pattern of black segregation.

One has to go back twenty years and get a sense of the period to make the case that at the time these views seemed justifiable, that there was good reason to believe that the remarkable revolution in civil rights law of the 1960s would spur the improvement in the economic, educational, housing, and neighborhood conditions of American blacks that had to a substantial degree already been evident in the postwar period.

Ben Wattenberg and others at the time published articles demonstrating the increased percentage of blacks becoming middle-class in occupation and earnings.[4] Irving Kristol had written an article in 1966, "The Negro Today Is Like the Immigrant Yesterday," a title which would strike us now with a certain irony, but which then made perfect sense.[5] It made sense to me. I had implied the same in *Beyond the Melting Pot*, in 1963.[6] Of course when we spoke of immigrants in the mid-1960s we weren't thinking about *new* immigrants to the United States—we were comparing Negroes to the immigrants of the past. Despite the passage of an immigration reform act in 1965, the immigrants were then people of yesterday, and no one expected that mass immigration to the United States would resume in the future.

One had reason in 1966, or ten years later, to expect that American Negroes, as they were then called, would follow the course of previous European immigrants, the "tenement trail," as Sam Lubell

▲ ▲ ▲

called it.[7] After all, American Negroes were still relative newcomers, compared with European immigrants, in the cities of the North and West, and now that we had powerful civil rights legislation, what would prevent their rise?

There were advocates for further massive federal measures, greater than those already in place, in education, housing, employment training, income support, and other areas to improve conditions in cities and for American blacks, but we were already in a period of federal (and state and local) fiscal constraint, from which we have never emerged. There had in any case already been a great expansion of federal programs in the 1960s and '70s. Thus, in the field of housing segregation alone, the Fair Housing Act of 1968 had been supplemented in 1974 by a Housing and Community Development Act that required communities to prepare a detailed "housing assistance plan," taking account of the needs of low-income families, before receiving federal grants. The Equal Credit Opportunity Act of 1974 prohibited discrimination in home lending and required banks to compile information on the race of loan applicants and recipients. A 1976 court order required three federal agencies to collect racial data on home loan applicants, and the 1975 Home Mortgage Disclosure Act required banks to report on the neighborhood pattern of their loans. The 1977 Community Reinvestment Act required banks to demonstrate that they were providing loans to low-income areas; and one could undoubtedly add other measures.

Was more necessary to assist the rise of blacks? Twenty years ago, one could believe, and I did believe, that more was not necessary—that the measures banning discrimination in employment, education, housing, government programs, were sufficient, that the agencies policing these measures were competent, that the civil rights groups watching the agencies were vigilant, that the courts which would respond to their complaints on effectiveness of enforcement were sympathetic. One could believe that American blacks would follow the path of European immigrants, now that state-imposed restrictions were lifted and private discrimination in key areas was banned.

Others did believe that more was necessary, and Anthony Downs was among them. The federal government was then engaged, as it still is, in efforts to go beyond the banning of overt and direct discrimination. We had extensive efforts at integration—in employment, through affirmative action; in education, through cases calling for desegregation through busing; in housing, where various schemes and programs were afoot to better integrate publicly subsidized housing and to require integration in private development. To such intrusive measures of integration I was opposed, and I expressed this opposition in *Affirmative Discrimination.* The European immigrants had not needed them, I argued, and American blacks would not need them as their educational attainment increased, their earnings rose, and they entered white-collar and professional and managerial occupations in greater numbers. Integration in schools and colleges and in housing and residence would follow in due course.

There was a good deal of ignorance of the ethnic and racial patterns of American life, I asserted, in those who saw every degree of separation of blacks from whites as the result of prejudice and discrimination, and set as the proper measure of equality the even distribution of blacks in all areas of life. There was an equal measure of ignorance of our ethnic and racial history among those who assumed that the break-up of concentrations by government action was necessary for black advancement. No ethnic or racial group had shown such an "even distribution." Black concentrations could have been matched by Jewish or Italian concentrations earlier in the century. In every group there was some tendency to prefer propinquity to family and friends and churches and social institutions. Differences in tastes and culture, as well as differences in income, led to a different pattern of institutional facilities and local

▲ ▲ ▲

businesses in residential neighborhoods. Many factors quite independent of prejudice and discrimination made some clustering of ethnic and racial groups inevitable and indeed natural. A decent respect for freedom of association and for the differences among people should be observed by government, and it should stand back from efforts to push the desired objective of integration. Integration would happen in any case, as a result of economic, political, and social changes that were inevitable.

These views, whatever evidence could have been collected to support them in the middle 1970s, now strike me as complacent. Some of these expected changes did take place. But the one area in which my seemingly reasonable expectations have remained unrealized has been housing and residential integration, and, as a consequence, school integration. The mid-1970s now emerge as a turning point, in which progress, by various measures—such as percentages of blacks going on to college, percentage in poverty— slowed down or stopped.[8] Why the improvement evident after World War II did not continue into the 1980s and '90s is not easy to explain. Of course by some measures there has been continuous improvement in the condition of American blacks. The number elected to public offices has continued to increase, as has the percentage moving into white collar and managerial occupations. But on other fronts the expected improvements did not take place or showed the most minimal change. Among these were measures of residential and school integration.

The American blacks, it turned out, were not like the immigrants of yesterday, or like the immigrants of today who have become so numerous in the wake of immigration reform in 1965. These are differences that must concern us, and lead us to think seriously again about why, thirty years after the great breakthrough in civil rights legislation, and despite the massive and revolutionary change in the attitudes of the American public, we are still, in some key respects, two nations. Consequences flow from that separation

▲ ▲ ▲

which continue to widen our differences, despite all the effort and all the change that should have led us to expect their narrowing. On these differences one could present a host of statistics. I will refer to only three phenomena which to me are peculiarly symptomatic of our situation.

Concerning one we hear little, and indeed it is not much studied: intermarriage. Intermarriage may well be considered the last step in assimilation. Sociologists have so considered it. After we become ready to work in politics together, to go to school together, to earn our living together, to live together in the same communities, and to go through the other stages which mark the overcoming of separation and difference between two groups, it is not surprising that this increasing togetherness should lead for many to intermarriage. Intermarriage is so crucial a final step because it does more than mark the attraction between two individuals—it marks the highest degree of social acceptance. One is almost embarrassed to present this sociological bromide, but one must justify bringing in intermarriage as a significant element in judging the quality of relations between races and ethnic groups. After all, is not equality in political rights, education, earnings, housing, sufficient? Why bring in this most intimate of social ties? One does because it is an indication that everything else in bringing groups together is working.

Blacks stand out uniquely in the array of American ethnic and racial groups in the degree to which marriage remains within the group. Among European ethnic groups, as we are well aware, intermarriage has blurred boundaries to the point where ethnic identity has become, for increasing numbers of Americans, a matter of choice as to which among a number of ancestries they shall choose to identify with, if any. This is the import of the work of Richard Alba and Mary Waters.[9] While ethnic identity—or the choice of an ethnic identity for one or another purpose—will go on for a long time, it will become more and more elusive.

▲ ▲ ▲

The group that has been most distinctive in maintaining its ethnic identity, one sustained not only by a common history but by a distinctive religion, bolstered by a unique tragedy, and guarded by a strong social and religious reluctance to accept intermarriage, is American Jews. But even they show an intermarriage rate among current marriages of 50 percent or more.[10] Sociologists and demographers who study American Jews now must take account of a growing penumbra of non-Jews and part-Jews who live in Jewish (and non-Jewish) households. This penumbra can only grow, to the point where, in a few generations, American Jews will be reduced to a resistant core and a growing surround of persons with some Jewish ancestry and some Jewish identity. (Of course all projections of this sort are to be understood with the caveat, "If no major counterforces intervene.")

For other European ethnic groups, rates of intermarriage are much higher than among Jews. The intermarriage rates for Asian and Hispanic groups, large percentages of whom are recent immigrants who we would expect to be most deeply rooted within their group in language, custom, and culture, are also surprisingly high. Various studies show current intermarriage rates of 30 percent or higher for the past twenty years.[11]

Where do blacks stand? According to data from the 1980 Census reported by Stanley Lieberson and Mary Waters, 98.7 percent of black native-born women marry other blacks.[12] By comparison, in-marriage among women of Puerto Rican ancestry is 78.7 percent, and for Mexican American women it is 76 percent. For European groups, old and new, the figures are under 50 percent, generally far under. Black men, especially those outside the South, marry outside their group more often than do black women, and recent studies show a steady rise in out-marriage in the last few decades.[13] But even with black male intermarriage rates outside the South of about 10 percent, the overall pattern is distinct and unique: Blacks, who are not an immigrant group (though a rising

percentage are indeed recent immigrants), who have been resident
on this soil for more generations than most white Americans, or
Hispanic Americans, or Asian Americans, are uniquely separated
from other Americans by this measure of integration.

A second measure which shows a unique degree of separation,
as we have said, is the residential concentration of blacks. The facts
have been developed most starkly and presented most effectively
by Douglas Massey and Nancy Denton in *American Apartheid*.[14]
Thirty years after the civil rights revolution and the revolutionary
change in the legal posture affecting discrimination, the situation
can only be described as extremely depressing. The authors develop measures of both "segregation" and "isolation," calculated on
different bases and reflecting somewhat different realities, but the
picture for both indices reflects so high a degree of separation that
it is hardly necessary to go into the details.

Comparing 1970 and 1980, they write: "Among the oldest and
largest northern ghettoes . . . there was virtually no sign of progress
in residential integration. In Boston, Chicago, Cleveland, Detroit,
Gary, Philadelphia, Pittsburgh and St. Louis, the decline in the
segregation index was 4 points or less, and in two metropolitan
areas (New York and Newark) segregation actually *increased* over
the decade." There were more substantial declines in Columbus,
Los Angeles, and San Francisco, but they attribute these declines
to "unusual instability in housing patterns caused by a combination
of gentrification, immigration, and rapid housing construction
rather than to an ongoing process of neighborhood racial integration."[15]

All the more benign explanations of this remarkable stability of
racial segregation collapse on investigation. Is this the pattern we
might expect from new immigrants or new migrants into cities?
Recency of migration does not explain it: Black communities in the
North and West are no longer fed by heavy immigration from the
South, and this has been the case for twenty years or more. Nev-

ertheless, the authors tell us, the levels of segregation in northern
cities in 1980 were above the highest ever recorded for European
ethnic groups.

Is this the same pattern we find for other nonwhite groups; is it
a general "minority" pattern? As in the case of intermarriage, it is
not: "The high level of segregation experienced by blacks today is
. . . unique compared with the experience of other large minority
groups, such as Hispanics and Asians." Black residential isolation
is as out of line compared with Asian or Hispanic patterns as is
black intermarriage.

Is this only a central city pattern, and can we expect its mitiga-
tion as more blacks move into suburbs? Perhaps we can, but black
suburbanization increases very slowly. The overwhelming majority
of blacks are still in central cities. Insofar as suburbanization has
increased, much of it has been into suburban areas that are in effect
extensions of central-city black areas, or into suburbs that have
become dominantly black. Black segregation is lower when we
consider the suburban areas of metropolitan areas as a whole, but
not markedly lower.

Is this pattern mitigated for blacks of higher income? Not at all.
Segregation is as severe for those with incomes above $50,000 as
for those below.

Is it the effect of black desires, black tastes? Do blacks prefer to
live in black areas? Not really. Blacks have been asked in public
opinion surveys what kind of neighborhood they would prefer to
live in: "By large majorities, blacks support the ideal of integration
and express a preference for integrated living and 95% are willing
to live in neighborhoods that are anywhere between 15% and 70%
black."[16]

But here we do have a problem in the interaction between black
desires as to the level of integration blacks would find comfortable
or prefer and the level whites would find comfortable or prefer.
Massey and Denton report that many surveys show that "blacks

strongly prefer a 50–50 mixture, and that whites have little tolerance for racial mixture beyond 20% black." The relationship between these preferences results in instability. I am not suggesting
that the proportion of black and white in a neighborhood is the
only factor or even necessarily the decisive factor in decisions to
move out of or move into a neighborhood. But in a society of high
mobility such as ours, with almost one-fifth of the households of the
country moving every year, even a modest preference in the residential racial mix desired will, over time, lead to a concentration of
blacks in one or a few areas.

Thomas Schelling elegantly demonstrated this twenty-five years
ago.[17] Take a checkerboard, he said, and distribute nickels and
dimes on it at random, with 10 percent of the coins nickels, and a
few spaces empty. Then move one coin at a time into an empty
space, with only this rule: The nickel would like to have at least one
of its neighboring spaces occupied by a nickel, the dime would like
to have one of its neighboring spaces occupied by a dime. In a
relatively few moves, the nickels begin to concentrate in one section of the checkerboard. If the preference is for two neighboring
nickels, or two neighboring dimes, the concentration will occur
faster.

But what underlies this process? To Massey and Denton, it is
prejudice. To me, the matter is more complicated. It is preference,
based on a range of factors. In some cases, particularly in white
working-class neighborhoods, we will indeed find prejudice, intense and direct. This is well documented in studies of such neighborhoods, but one scarcely needs the studies—the newspaper
reports are enough.[18] This prejudice is based to some degree on the
experience of such communities with low-income blacks in their
neighborhoods. It is not easy to separate out from prejudice the
influence of fears that, with an increase in black occupancy, crime
will increase, schools will decline, and house values will drop. In
enlightened middle-class neighborhoods, with a commitment to the

▲ ▲ ▲

ideal of integration, the fears of what kind of change will occur with an increase in black occupancy may have little to do with prejudice, as ordinarily understood. But in these neighborhoods there will also be fears that crime will increase, property values will decline, schools will become poorer.[19] These fears are shared by both blacks and whites. There is little difference between blacks and whites in their expectation that more blacks will mean more crime, a decline in property values.

Whether low-income or middle-income, prejudiced or unprejudiced, neighborhoods will organize, using different methods and appeals, to restrain an increase in black occupancy. When houses are the largest part of the wealth of a family, it is understandable homeowners will act with as much caution as bondholders, who are ready to move billions on the basis of fears that to many of us appear minuscule.

The Schelling demonstration, the fact that small preferences, or, if you will, a relatively modest degree of prejudice, may produce large effects, may save American society from the charge of being irredeemably racist, but the consequences, in terms of separation and segregation, seem to be remarkably similar. Working-class attitudes may be more prejudiced than middle-class attitudes (in any case, the expression of prejudice is more direct and unmodulated), but behavior will still aim at either exclusion of blacks or the restriction of black entry, often leading, if restriction fails, to the rapid turnover of an area to almost totally black. The sharp decline in the racist sentiments of the American population in the past thirty years—and I do not dismiss this decline as simply a matter of being polite and proper to the opinion pollsters—has done remarkably little to change the overall pattern of black concentration, of black isolation from the rest of the population. Schelling's demonstration explains in part why such a sharp decline in negative attitudes can have such modest effects on the overall pattern of segregation, but the segregation remains.

And it has, I believe, serious consequences, even though social scientists continue to debate whether there is a "contagion" effect, whether the indices of dysfunction among the black poor would be the same or different if they were spread out and integrated rather than concentrated and isolated.[20] Just how to sort out the influences that make the black inner-city ghetto what it is today is not simple. Poverty? Lack of jobs? Lack of role models? Concentration? Poor schools? The possibilities are endless. Yet it stands to reason that if the black poor could be redistributed so that their neighbors, black or white, were often not poor, it would help. There is some research evidence, as we will see, that common sense on this matter is not mistaken, but whatever the more sophisticated research concludes, most of us will believe the segregation of the black poor in the central cities has serious consequences. Those behaviors with which we are all familiar from television and the newspapers—a high rate of crime, juvenile delinquency, poor school performance, out-of-wedlock births, and the rest—must be accentuated by the effect of concentration alone, even though social scientists are not yet agreed that they can demonstrate this independent effect.

A third aspect of the separation of the races is its effects on language and, at the extremes, the capacity to communicate. Of course any group develops a distinctive vocabulary, idioms, formulations, intonations, but the black poor seem to be drifting further away from standard English, very likely an effect of isolation and concentration, and this adds an additional burden to the efforts to break out of the ghetto and poverty.

For the most part blacks and whites understand one another well enough, across the barriers of race and class. But a different style of English, particularly if it is associated with a historically lower caste, communicates something as to class, attitude, community, and a host of other factors which add up to a sense of difference, and the kind of difference that suggests the possibility of trouble to the dominant caste. Despite the overwhelming presence of the mass media, the speech variants drift further apart. It seems speech patterns are communicated better orally by one's close associates from childhood, with whom one is in direct face-to-face contact, than by the TV set or the newspaper or the school. As a leading sociolinguist, William Labov, writes on the basis of studies in Philadelphia and elsewhere: "The black population does not participate in the rapid evolution of the white vernacular . . . As the sound pattern of the Philadelphia white community becomes more and more different from the speech of Boston, Chicago and Fort Worth, it is also becoming more and more different from the sound pattern used by black Philadelphians. We find the same situation in all the large Northern cities . . . The local white accents show rapid divergence from each other, while the black communities remain aloof. Instead of increased differentiation, the black sound pattern shows a generalized Northern black phonology."[21]

This research on language is intriguing, but a resort to common experience on this point is as persuasive. Thirty years after the great effort in public law to bring us together, does one detect any lessening of the distinctive patterns of black English among the black poor, among the young blacks often featured in television programs on one or another social or educational problem? If anything, they are maintained and strengthened. A related phenomenon is the well-documented pattern in black ghetto schools of hostility to academic achievement; it is considered "acting white." Speaking the common English of the TV anchor would also be considered "acting white." These behaviors are undoubtedly spurred by ideological changes, by the shift in the attitudes of black leadership, and blacks generally, away from the assumption that blacks should act more like whites in order to progress toward the goal of assimilation. Instead we find support for various degrees of distinctiveness and difference, and the rise of a distinctive black identity in which the abandonment of linguistic distinctiveness may be seen as a form of group betrayal. This will be interpreted differently at different class levels, and the signs of continuing group solidarity will vary enormously as one moves from ghetto youths to corporate lawyers. But even in the most elite groups, some sign of linguistic distinctiveness, however etiolated, is commonly maintained.

Separation, as well as differences in interest, contributes to blacks and whites coming to see the world differently. The surprisingly large divergence that was shown in public opinion polls between blacks and nonblacks as to O. J. Simpson's guilt is only the most striking of these differences in how blacks and whites see the world. (It was driven home to whites in the course of this trial what good reasons blacks had to view the police and the system of justice differently from whites.) Recently it has been noted that black and white television viewers are growing further apart in the programs they favor. Separation in residence and schooling is only one factor leading to these different interests and orientations. It turns out that TV producers are seeking to appeal to niche audiences, particularly if they form very large niches, as is the case with blacks, who watch television more than whites. As the reporter of this phenomenon writes, "The change is driven as much by the competitive pressures that networks are feeling as any social or cultural factors, TV executives and others say."[22] Blacks and whites may have different views even when they live next door to each other, but I believe residential and school isolation makes a considerable contribution to these stark differences in outlook.

It is at this point, when we lay out the facts that cannot be explained away, and when we lay out the consequences, about which we can still argue, that the difficult part begins. What is to be done? Can anything be done? Should anything be done? If under a regime of freedom in which racial discrimination is banned and often punished, blacks remain separate from whites, might that not be an indication of the fact that over these twenty years the

desire to retain something distinctive that characterizes blacks—
differences that have been created by a tragic history but which
despite that have become valued signs of identity—has grown?
The black of today is not the immigrant of yesterday (or of today,
who assimilates probably at the same rate as the immigrants of
yesterday). To many blacks, a high degree of separation in intermarriage, residence, and language may describe a faultline in
American society that is a social reality rather than a problem. This
is one possible way of interpreting and responding to these facts.

If indeed that separation was chosen by those who have the
opportunity and ability to choose otherwise, then there might be
nothing more to say. Conceivably we might view the separation of
blacks from whites the way we view the separation from the larger
society of the Amish or of Hasidic Jews. But the comparison is
specious. When we speak of blacks, we are speaking of a group
that is one-eighth of American society, not a tiny minority, and a
group that is deeply implicated in the central themes of our history.
Its major figures have always fought for integration into American
life, whatever the power of separatist thinking among some members of the black community. Black separatism is largely a reaction
to what is seen as white rejection, of the failure of the larger society
to integrate blacks.

Separation is not for the most part voluntarily chosen. It is the
product of the interaction of poverty, social dysfunction, and the
reaction of others to these problems. Separateness among middle-
class blacks, whether self-selected or the product of that subtle
interaction of differences in taste that Schelling analyzed, would be
a different, and lesser, problem than the involuntary separateness
of the black poor.

We should also not exaggerate the degree of this separation. The
"segregation" index (which "gives the percentage of all blacks who
would have to move to achieve an even . . . residential configura-
tion—where each census tract replicates the racial composition of

the metropolitan area as a whole") for the thirty metropolitan areas with the largest black populations averages 80.1 for the North and West, 68.3 for the South in 1980.[23] This shows some degree of integration, and some change since 1970, from averages of 84.5 and 75.3, respectively. The "isolation" indices, which "state the percentage of blacks living in the tract of the average African-American" and "measure the extent to which blacks live only among other blacks and gauge the potential for interracial contact within neighborhoods," are considerably lower, especially outside the South — 66.1 in the North and West, 63.5 in the South.[24]

Perhaps one could argue on the basis of these figures that one-third of blacks are residentially integrated. Other data suggest a degree of integration that is considerably greater. Surprisingly, "almost 80 percent of blacks claim 'a good friend' who is white, and high-status blacks are especially likely to make such claims," according to a survey by the National Conference of Christians and Jews.[25] In contrast, the reality of our inner cities, and these need not be very large cities, informs us, independently of indices, that the degree of separation of blacks is unique in our culture. Twenty years ago we thought the increase in the education and income and occupational level of blacks, as long as we policed against discrimination, would ameliorate the problem, and we would end up with degrees of concentrations of blacks no greater than that we could see among other groups in the American ethnic and racial flux. It didn't happen.

Proposing activist policies to promote integration is generally the way in which such a discussion ends. That is the way Anthony Downs ended *Opening Up the Suburbs* twenty years ago, and that is the way Massey and Denton end *American Apartheid*. But such proposals exude an air of futility even as they are proposed. Whatever the policy, we have had some experience with it and know the inherent difficulties. One can require public housing agencies to have policies of racial integration. One can require that new private developments put aside a certain percentage of units for low-income families or for blacks, and these requirements can be variously federal, state, local, judicial. One can require banks to provide more mortgages for blacks to buy in nonblack areas. One can require secondary mortgage agencies to pressure those banks to provide more mortgages for blacks to buy in nonblack areas. One can require government oversight agencies to monitor secondary mortgage agencies' pressure on banks to issue more mortgages for blacks to buy in nonblack areas. And so on and so on. One can be very ingenious in finding ways in which government, involved in so many parts of our lives, can bring its power into effect to encourage integration. A whole vocabulary has grown up around such efforts.[26]

But even as one spells out the litany of possible activist interventions, the accompanying objections and problems and difficulties in implementing them unrolls before the eye of anyone who has had any experience with these efforts. As in the case of school busing, partially implemented, doubtfully successful, and now increasingly abandoned, government measures inspired by an ideal of fairness, equality, and integration cannot overcome the stubborn commitments of parents to what they consider best for their own children and neighborhood. Against these bedrock sentiments, all of government's good intentions, all well-designed public policies, crumble.

And even the best of these may have negative consequences. Efforts to integrate public housing projects have frequently placed elderly whites (because other poor whites were not available) next door to young black families, which has provided a difficult environment for the elderly and only reinforced their prejudices against blacks. Sometimes when private developers of rental projects have made special efforts to recruit white tenants in order to maintain an integrated community, they have been sued by the NAACP or the government for discriminating against blacks. This is what happened to Starrett City in Brooklyn.[27] If liberal suburban neighbor-

▲ ▲ ▲

hoods, seeing a slow drift to black majority residence, make special efforts to recruit white families when houses becomes available, by advertising their community to whites and creating programs to assist white families to move in, how different from discrimination will that appear to civil rights agencies or indeed black neighbors? Neither black civil rights organizations nor government agencies may be willing to make the distinction between "discriminating against" and trying to maintain "integration with," and indeed the distinction is not easy to make: Activist community efforts to maintain an integrated community require discrimination.

There are creative programs: Guaranteeing to white homeowners that the value of their property will not fall, for example. But how different is that from discrimination? And how extensive can such programs be, and how effective, when homeowners hope for unrealistic increases in the value of their property?

In Boston in the 1970s the mayor and the banks agreed to make a major commitment to provide below-rate mortgages to blacks moving into a then-white middle- and lower-income homeowning community. A Jewish neighborhood was selected for this large program, to reduce the chances of violence against entering blacks. The primary objective was improving housing conditions among blacks, but certainly there was no expectation the neighborhood would go all black—integration was also the goal. But then real estate agents moved in, frightening the whites in the neighborhood, urging them to get out fast before blacks moved in, and pressuring black families to take mortgages they could not afford. One can spell out the rest. The neighborhood declined rapidly; the ghetto expanded.[28] Perhaps the program was implemented poorly, but one cannot deny the good intentions. Even the somewhat suspicious chroniclers and analysts of this debacle accept that there were good intentions.

Whatever the virtue of these and other policies—and their virtues are to be found generally more in the intentions of their implementers than in their effects—who can expect them to be adopted on any large scale in the present political mood, or indeed in any foreseeable future political mood? The two Democratic administrations that have been inserted into decades of Republican presidential dominance have been understandably more sympathetic to such measures than the Republican administrations, but very little has been accomplished. The history of policy efforts to integrate neighborhoods and communities has been one of many schemes, and extended and endless litigation, and very small successes.

And yet there have been successes, small-scale, painful, often expensive, in the maintenance of integrated residential neighborhoods, generally upper-middle-class, and in some programs to move central-city blacks out of concentrated areas. Richard Taub and his collaborators have documented some of the former in Chicago, a highly segregated city.[29] We have seen similar efforts with variable success in the St. Louis and Cleveland areas and elsewhere.[30] But Taub also documents how perilous, how much on the edge, these successes are, if the measure is the maintenance of integration. They have often required heavy institutional commitments, such as those by the University of Chicago, and such actors are only available in some neighborhoods. They are assisted by the inherent attractiveness of housing in some neighborhoods—and this generally means older housing, built at a time when size and ornament and craftsmanlike elaboration characterized urban housing for the upper-middle class. Such neighborhoods are not to be found in profusion either.

Those engaged in the effort to maintain these integrated neighborhoods must fight often against civil rights groups who see discrimination in the effort to attract or assist new white residents (which it is, in the strict sense) and against militant groups who claim that "gentrification" is driving out the poor, even when such neighborhoods are marked by abandoned and under-used housing. What one learns from such neighborhood stories is that the effort to maintain integration must be just that, an effort, without assured success.

If an area is located far from expanding black areas, if the values of its properties are high, integration does not necessarily mean increasing fear of crime, value decline, and neighborhood deterioration. There are hundreds of such areas, unremarked and unrecorded in the sociological literature, and it is inevitable there will be more as the black middle class expands. Richard Nathan of the Nelson A. Rockefeller Institute of Government in Albany is now studying them, and his studies will reduce the dominant tendency to emphasize problems and may demonstrate how people with some resources following their interests naturally produce integration, the effect I expected twenty years ago. The environment of civil rights laws, of increasing opportunity and achievement for many blacks, and the change to more tolerant attitudes have had their effect. But the numbers of black families living in integrated circumstances is apparently relatively small, for the expansion of such areas makes no substantial impact on Massey's and Denton's measures. They show a glacial rate of change in segregation and isolation, though they mark some success in the integration of African Americans into American society.

Our attention however is concentrated, for good reason, on the isolation of the black poor. This is the "black ghetto," whose persistence has told us that the black of today, alas, whatever the cause, is not the immigrant of yesterday, or even the immigrant of today—who is less segregated and isolated than American blacks—but reflects a rather more profound divide in American society.

Here the prognosis is hardly encouraging. The leading candidate in the field of activist policy at the moment is the Gautreaux program in Chicago. Following lawsuits attacking the racial isolation in Chicago's public housing projects that went to the Supreme Court, a program has been implemented by the Department of

Housing and Urban Development in which 5,000 low-income families have been relocated into white suburban areas.[31] It seems successful, as measured by the ability to find suburban landlords who would accept subsidized inner-city female-headed families, by the recruitment of such families to make the move, by the content-ment of these families with their new houses and neighborhoods, by the effects on the children's education. The success of a program on such a scale has led Henry Cisneros, Secretary of Housing and Urban Development, to try to expand it, but that expansion is hostage to the fate of appropriations for the heavy housing subsi-dies that are required by the program.

In the end, whatever the good of the Gautreaux program, one is doubtful about its effects in bringing black and white together. Its scale can never match the huge size of the inner-city black ghettoes. Perhaps more important, it aims at bringing together the black poor, and generally the nonworking poor, in subsidized apartments and houses with the nonblack working and middle class. But that is trying to do too much. That indefatigable propo-nent of measures to advance integration, Anthony Downs, in 1973 coined the phrase to describe a more reasonable objective: "dis-persed economic integration."[32] This subtle phrase was meant to advise us that bringing together the races was hard enough without adding the further difficulty of bringing together the classes, something which the pattern of American urban develop-ment has never been good at doing. Our expectation has always been that the poor improve themselves by becoming less poor, and then by moving to the neighborhoods of the less poor, leaving the ghetto behind.[33] They do not characteristically improve themselves by inserting themselves into areas they cannot afford before their economic circumstances have improved—or worse, to describe Gautreaux properly, by being inserted, through government sub-sidies, into areas they cannot afford. To the cultural differences of race, not insubstantial, are then added the cultural differences of class. To expect this to work, to take this as a model, is to demand too much.

One could tell a similar story about our thirty-year-old effort to desegregate or racially integrate our schools. This effort has been frustrated primarily by the spatial separation of blacks and whites in our cities. If elementary public schools served the surrounding neighborhood, they inevitably were mostly black or white — "seg- regated," in the current lexicon. The only way of changing this was busing, to which parents expressed enormous resistance, either through direct confrontation, as in Boston, or more commonly by withdrawing their children from public schools or moving to areas with schools unaffected by busing. The resistance was attacked as racist, and often was, but it was also a reflection of parents' concern for the education and environment of their children, who, as is often pointed out, only go through school once. The opposition to busing also reflected a widespread indignation over a degree of governmental intervention that most people believed went too far. Busing was instituted in a large number of American cities, but with the increase of black school populations and the reduction in the white population of cities through suburbanization, it often became a futile exercise of moving black students from all-black schools to schools only marginally less black. Courts are now allowing cities to suspend busing for integration. We can tell suc- cess stories about busing, as we can about some efforts to integrate housing racially, but the successes have not affected the overall picture of separation.

If the schools were going to be all-black or mostly black, and if their teachers and administrators changed to reflect in some degree the changing school population, it was the most natural thing in the world that some cognizance would be taken of the race and presumed distinctive experience of the children. This was being done in many places long before the term "multiculturalism" was applied to it. The ground for multiculturalism in its more extensive form was prepared by the continuing separation of black and white, which has become increasingly, with the rise of the Hispanic and Asian population through immigration, the separation of black and nonblack. Mexican American and other Hispanic children are also highly concentrated in some schools, but we can attribute that concentration to the impact of immigration. It is not very different from the overwhelmingly Jewish or Italian schools of the age of mass immigration, and will last as long as immigration remains at a high level. The facts of declining residential separation and increasing intermarriage of second- and third-generation Hispanics tell us clearly that their degree of concentration is a first- and second-generation immigrant phenomenon. It is not the same story as the concentration or separation of blacks, which has been maintained centuries after they were brought to this country as slaves.

Government has been as ineffective in overcoming segregation at the elementary school level as it has been in overcoming the prevailing residential segregation, though government programs have tried to do so. Government action can never match, in scale and impact, the crescive effects of individual, voluntary decision. This is what has raised group after group in the past, this is what is breaking down the barriers of ethnicity and race today. But these effects have operated excruciatingly slowly when it comes to American blacks. They have operated to some extent, as we see by the greatly expanded number of blacks making middle-class incomes, by the creation of integrated middle-class neighborhoods. It is the rate of movement toward integration and the contrast with the patterns of immigrant groups that have been so disappointing. Why our expectations were so disappointed is still obscure, and all the research does not make it clearer. We have to go back to such factors as the disaster that encompassed the black family, the failure to close educational achievement gaps, the rise of worklessness among black males, the increase in crime—and behind all these there are other factors in infinite regress, among them prejudice and discrimination which, while declining, are still evident.

This failure leads many to propose larger-scale governmental action, unlikely as the prospects for such are in the present and foreseeable political climate. But even if that climate were better, it is hard to see what government programs could achieve. They would be opposed by the strongest motives that move men and women, their concern for family, children, property. However wrong I was in expecting more rapid change to result from the civil rights revolution, a greater measure of government effort to directly promote residential integration and school integration is not the answer. The forces that will produce the changes we are looking for are individual and voluntaristic, rather than governmental and authoritative. To adapt the title of Glenn Loury's book,[34] it will have to be "one by one," individual by individual, family by family, neighborhood by neighborhood. Slowly as these work, there is really no alternative.

In the meantime, there is multiculturalism.

8 ▲ ▲ ▲ ▲ ▲ ▲ ▲ ▲ ▲ ▲ ▲ ▲ ▲ ▲ ▲ ▲

"WE ARE ALL MULTICULTURALISTS NOW"

Multiculturalism is the price America is paying for its inability or unwillingness to incorporate into its society African Americans, in the same way and to the same degree it has incorporated so many groups.

Multiculturalism appears on the surface to encompass much more than that, and indeed it reflects and is responsive to a variety of other developments: the remarkable rise of the women's movement and women's studies, the change in sexual mores and morality which makes gays and lesbians a visible and open presence in culture, politics, and education, the impact of the new immigration, the declining self-confidence or arrogance of the United States as the best, as well as the richest and most powerful, country. All these play a role in how we conceive our past and our future, in how we educate our children, in how we speak to one another, and in how we conceive of the role of race and ethnicity in American society, government, and culture.

But the role of African Americans in multiculturalism is quite different from that of women, or gays and lesbians, or new immigrants, or Hispanics or Asians or Native Americans. No one has to

147

argue the primacy of the fate and history of American blacks among the forces making for multiculturalism in America—or so it would appear. But even those most sensitive to this issue, such as Todd Gitlin, are nevertheless overwhelmed by the flux of identities, and see that as the danger to a better life based on common values: "American culture in the late twentieth century is a very stewpot of separate identities. Not only blacks and feminists and gays declare that their dignity rests on their distinctness, but so in various ways do white Southern Baptists, Florida Jews, Oregon skinheads, Louisiana Cajuns, Brooklyn Lubavitchers, California Sikhs, Wyoming ranchers."[1]

True enough. There is evidence for all of this. The changes that increase the visibility, size, presence of so many of these groups are real, and we find their equivalents in many countries. But even the powerful women's movement pales in significance for the future of American society contrasted with the far greater separateness, the far greater weight of grievances, the far greater capacity to harm the common enterprise because of the distinctive condition and hurts, of American blacks.

We have changed sharply our ideas about the role of women in society, as they have moved into key professions in which they were once scarcely represented, as they have changed our language and our sense of the proper relations between the sexes. But the change that has taken place in our conception of how blacks would relate to the rest of American society is of quite a different order of magnitude. In the 1960s we—and in that "we" I include blacks and whites—thought that the future of American blacks would show a rapid increase in their income, their education, their participation as equals in American society, and their integration in our common society. Perhaps our ideas were not as clear as that, but no one expected the degree of separation in ways of life and thought that prevails in 1997. "The American dilemma" continues to refer to only one thing. It is not what place women should play in our

common life, though there are complicated and troubling issues
enough under that rubric.

If we were to read today Disraeli's comment on the England of
his day, "Two nations, between whom there is no intercourse and
no sympathy . . . ignorant of each other's habits . . . ordered by
different manners," we might perhaps think, as Disraeli intended,
of the rich and the poor, and of the increasing economic inequality
by some measures among Americans.[2] But in truth that does not
seem to affect our politics or our lives much. When we say today
in America that we are two nations, we mean what Andrew Hacker
meant when he titled his book *Two Nations: Black and White, Separate,
Hostile, Unequal.*[3]

The two nations for our America are the black and the white,
and increasingly, as Hispanics and Asians become less different
from whites from the point of view of residence, income, occupation, and political attitudes, the two nations become the black and
the others. The change that has shaken our expectations for the
future of American society is not the rise of women or of gays and
lesbians. It is rather the change in our expectations as to how and
when the full incorporation of African Americans into American
life will take place. Only twenty years ago we could still believe that
African Americans would become, in their ways of life, their degree
of success, their connection to society, simply Americans of darker
skin. I still believe that will happen eventually. But our progress in
moving toward that goal, while evident in some respects, shows
some serious backsliding, and more than that, a hard institutionali-
zation of differences, one example of which is multiculturalism in
American education. It is not easy to see how these institutionalized
differences will be overcome soon.

Those of us who were students of ethnicity and race in the 1960s,
and held the perspective that assimilation—or, if one prefers the
milder term, integration—was what happened to ethnic and racial
groups in America, could look unconcernedly on many of the signs

of continuing black separation and difference. Of course blacks
clustered together. But isn't this what all new immigrant and mi-
grant groups had done? Of course blacks on average earned less
than other Americans—but weren't there differences among all
racial and ethnic groups, depending on their specific histories? And
wouldn't these differences decline as an age of prejudice and discrimination and enforced separation became ever more distant? Of
course blacks organized politically around the issues that meant
most to them, and were appealed to by politicians on the basis of
their common race. But isn't that what had happened with all
ethnic and racial groups even while the forces of assimilation were
at work on them?

The middle years of this century saw the abolition of all limitations
in law on grounds of race and ethnicity. In his history of naturalization in the United States, Reed Ueda writes of the McCarran-Wal-
ter Act of 1952, at the time execrated because of its maintenance of
national quotas in immigration: "At one stroke the arbitrary category of 'aliens ineligible for citizenship,' which had consigned Asian
nationalities to the inferior status of permanent-resident aliens for a
century, was swept away." He concludes his authoritative account
of the history of American naturalization optimistically: "By the
mid-20th century the racial restrictions of naturalization [they had
never affected blacks] seemed impolitic and impractical. Experience
had shown that all ethnic groups, given time and encouragement,
had the capacity to assimilate into the national civic culture, and so
U.S. citizenship was opened to all . . . Fears that ethnocultural or
racial background would inhibit the proper exercise of citizenship
rights were supplanted by a confidence that citizenship was a tran-
scendent status obtainable by all individuals who shared a common
membership in a democratic polity."[4]

In 1964 a wide-reaching Civil Rights Act banned discrimination
on the basis of race or ethnicity or national origin in employment,
public facilities, education, government programs; in 1965 a pow-

▲ ▲ ▲

erful Voting Rights Act ensured access to the ballot and more, and an Immigration Reform Act eliminated national quotas. Twenty years ago, few would have challenged the notion that the expansion of American citizenship and the rights that came with it had overcome all racial and ethnic limitations to become universal in its reach. That's what American history taught us, and no one dreamed there could be any regress from the high points of the Civil Rights Act and the Immigration Act of 1964 and 1965. That was law; common practice might still be different, and whites, Christians, Protestants might still be favored in many areas of life, as they could not be favored in law. But how long would that last in the face of legal changes, and powerful agencies to enforce them? This was the period when, for example, anti-Semitism rapidly declined, and Jews were becoming for the first time presidents of major universities and CEOs of major corporations. This was also the period in which expressions of prejudice and practices of discrimination against blacks were rapidly declining. The anti-Japanese sentiments of World War II, indeed the anti-Asian sentiments epidemic in America since the mid-nineteenth century, were also in rapid decline. One could be optimistic that the last barriers to difference in treatment based on race, religion, nationality were being swept aside.

This was the point of view I expressed in a book of 1975, *Affirmative Discrimination*.[5] It was within that circle of change and expectation that the book criticized affirmative action in employment, then still in the first few years of its development, as well as busing for the racial integration of schools, and housing policies that imposed requirements to achieve a target racial mix in housing. All these, it seemed to me, were unnecessary in view of what was happening to American attitudes, and transgressed the spirit and specific provisions of the Civil Rights Act of 1964. The first chapter of the book laid out the basis of this criticism of the new race-conscious policies by arguing that the spirit of the American

Revolution and our founding documents aimed at this ultimate color-blindness, whatever the limitations that had hindered the fulfillment of this aim for two centuries.

We know that when Jefferson wrote "all men are created equal," slavery existed, there was legal discrimination against Jews and Catholics, American Indians were outside the polity, and if there had been any Asians or Hispanics around at the time there would undoubtedly have been discrimination against them, too. But, I asserted, with more boldness and self-confidence than I would today, the spirit of our culture and polity made all these anomalies that would in time be eliminated. The pattern of American history steadily moved us to a more expansive notion of the "American," to reach the final culmination of 1964 and 1965.

But what does one mean when one makes such claims for "the spirit of our culture," "the pattern of our history"? Who can pronounce on these with confidence? In *Affirmative Discrimination* I drew on some leading authorities on the development of American nationality and American national ideals: Seymour Martin Lipset, in his 1963 book, *The First New Nation;* Hans Kohn in his 1957 *American Nationalism: An Interpretation;* Yehoshua Arieli, in his 1964 *Individualism and Nationalism in American Ideology.* All three were quite confident that the pattern of American history showed this tendency toward greater inclusion or equality from its origins, and that the facts that indicated otherwise were anomalies that would in time be swept aside, as indeed was happening.

These days, critics of this argument would probably note, if they were unkind enough, that my three chief authorities were a child of immigrants, a refugee, and an Israeli, all Jews, who understandably might take this generous view of the course and aims of American history (as I, the child of Jewish immigrants, would too). It was not long after the publication of *Affirmative Discrimination* that Ronald Takaki strongly attacked this optimistic view of the pattern and direction of American history in its treatment of the foreigner, the nonwhite, the other, as it is now put. He had plenty of quotations from founding fathers to set against those that Lipset, Kohn, and Arieli (and I, following them) had recorded to defend our optimistic views on the inclusion of the nonwhite and non-European in American society and polity.[6]

It seemed there could be very wide divergence in how to interpret the pattern of American history. Originally this divergence was surprising to me, and possibly to the main body of interpreters of American history and society. Who could dispute in 1965, or in 1975, the viewpoint that the Civil Rights Act and Immigration Act of 1964 and 1965 marked a permanent advance to full inclusiveness? That challenge became easier to pose over time, and has climaxed in the dispute over multiculturalism.

The weight of that challenge came home to me at one point in the course of the discussions of the New York State committee on the social studies curriculum (see Chapter 2). While searching for an appropriately broad-based and general statement to help us introduce our recommendations, I came across a statement in a report by the Curriculum Task Force of the National Commission on Social Studies in the Schools, which was composed of leading historians and teachers of social studies and which seemed to me sound and unassailable. It read:

Classrooms today bring together young people of many backgrounds with a broad spectrum of life experience. We can expect an even more diverse student population in the twenty-first century. This diversity enriches our nation even as it presents a new challenge to develop the social studies education that integrates all students into our system of democratic government and helps them subscribe to the values from our past—especially our devotion to democratic values and procedures. The coexistence of increasing diversity and cherished tradition require social studies in our schools to cultivate participatory citizenship . . . The study of social involvement and often competing loyalties addresses basic questions: "Who am I?" "To what communities do I belong?" "What does citizenship in our nation require of me as an individual and as a member of the various groups to which I belong?"[7]

I will admit I was astonished when the co-chairman of our small committee of two which had been assigned the task of writing the introductory statement for our report, a Hispanic scholar, vigorously objected to the use of these to me unobjectionable and bland statements. To him, they suggested that "there is a fund of common values in the U.S. that should be imposed on all immigrants." He thought the contrast between "increasing diversity" and "cherished traditions" "uncharitable." He felt the use of the word "ours" was exclusionary. He saw in the statement the "xenophobic language of the nativists and the Americanization movement," of "the worst moments of U.S. chauvinism." He objected that the reference to "competing loyalties" depreciated the significance of group distinctiveness and group loyalty for minority groups. I interpret this objection to mean that he refused to place subgroup loyalty on the same level as a larger American loyalty. Subgroup loyalty rather trumped American loyalty. He feared the "retreat of the Euro-American minority [he is referring to the time when the Euro-Americans will become a minority] from the cherished guarantees found in the Constitution."

How broadly these sentiments would be held among Hispanic Americans, or Hispanic American scholars, I do not know. There is no necessary equivalence between a person's race or ethnicity and the views that person holds. It is one of the errors of the more extreme versions of multiculturalism to believe there is. But these suspicions are not simply personal, or isolated among intellectuals and academics. There is enough evidence that among one group in the American population they are widespread indeed, and lead to a radically different outlook on American history and society from

▲ ▲ ▲

the outlook commonly found not only among European Americans but, I would warrant, among Hispanic and Asian Americans, too. The group in which we find this radical divergence from the norm is American blacks, and it is matched by a radical difference, on the average, in living conditions from that found among most other Americans.

As we saw when we looked at the history of assimilation and discrimination (in Chapter 6), and at the distinctive residential patterns of blacks, maintained through decades when prejudice and discrimination declined and was banned in law, when we considered the unique black exception from the prevailing patterns of intergroup marriage, and the maintenance and perhaps exaggeration of dialectal variations which are given significant cultural and political meaning (Chapter 7), the situation of African Americans is different. Of course all groups are different. There were significant differences in the ways European immigrant groups assimilated. But there are orders of magnitude in difference. The differences between the rate of assimilation of Irish and Germans, or Italians and Jews, become quite small when we contrast them with the differences over time between white European immigrants of any group and American blacks. These differences create different perspectives, on our historic past, on our present, on the shape of our culture.

Very likely, in view of all the other changes that have affected American society in the past twenty years, we would have seen multiculturalism of some form affecting American education, whatever the degree to which the common expectations regarding black assimilation were realized. After all, even homogeneous European countries, with no equivalent in their history of the deep division between majority and minority that characterizes the United States, have their various versions of multiculturalism, and make use of the same term.

But this term does not have, cannot have, the weight in Britain, France, Germany, or Sweden that it has in the United States. For these countries, multiculturalism means the more or less grudging acknowledgment that they will have to bring into line with their principles, which are the increasingly universal Western principles of the equal worth of all men and women, some of their common public and private practices, in the provision of social services, in schooling, in housing, in patterns of hiring and promotion. They will have to deal with and modify an often matter-of-fact discrimination based on the unquestioned reality that the people of these countries have been for centuries dominantly of one linguistic and cultural group, sharing some degree of suspicion of and distaste for outsiders. These countries have been reminded by their own scholars that they have in the past incorporated larger numbers of immigrants than they were aware of, and that in the world of the late twentieth century the pattern of incorporation of new immigrants will have to be somewhat different from what it was in the nineteenth and earlier twentieth centuries, the ages of European self-confidence and evident superiority. They will have to pay somewhat more attention to difference, will have to be more tolerant of the institutions created by new groups that maintain difference.

This is not to say there are no serious problems for this new European multiculturalism, in particular those raised by large resident Muslim communities. Islam, for complicated historical reasons, has chosen to emphasize its differences with Western liberalism. It therefore becomes a potentially rebellious element within Western societies, and in so becoming creates dilemmas for them in their commitment to liberal values. Separate schools for Jews, Catholics, Protestants, or atheists seem to pose no great problem for the dominantly liberal societies of Western Europe. Separate schools for Muslims do, primarily because, in their attitudes toward women and heterodoxy, they sharply challenge liberal values. So the acceptance of difference, in the case of Islam, poses a serious problem for liberal values, as is the case whenever a liberal society confronts a group that rejects the very values that undergird the support of difference. This is the central issue that a resurgent Islam raises for liberal Western societies. It is serious enough.

It is, however, quite different from the issues raised by African Americans, who have been closely bound up with white Americans since the time of the founding of the English colonies of the Atlantic coast. The only possible comparison with Europe would be if the Saxons of England, or the Gauls of France, had been held in a position of caste subservience for centuries. This kind of split, sunk deep in the history of societies, does not exist in Europe. We believed in the 1960s that our founding principles, elaborated as they had been over two centuries until they reached the all-embracing form of the civil rights and immigration legislation of the 1960s, would serve to overcome this deep fissure in our own society. Our history, after all, has been one of an increasingly expansive liberalism in our conception of who is legitimately American, an increasing effectiveness in bringing groups ever more distant from the founding stock into full membership in American polity and society.

We were in our origins dominantly of English stock, along with less numerous groups from Northwestern Europe, of various Protestant religions, and including a large minority of black slaves. There was, fortunately, no formal and binding recognition of these origins in our major founding legal documents. Because we were establishing our independence in revolt against a nation of the same stock, and because of our anxiety about favoring one Protestant church or sect over another, our founding documents are cast in general terms, appealing to universal principles. Whatever the practices of exclusion—and they were many—they were in time (and not without backsliding) steadily reduced. The eligibility of all the world to become Americans on an equal basis with all others was regularly asserted by American presidents, regardless of party and ideology.

Practice in all the spheres of American life was expected to follow, and in large measure it has. No one can ignore the remarkable transformation in the role of African Americans in the South, and the changes in their position in many sectors of American society.

But we also cannot ignore the remarkable and unique degree of separation between blacks and others. The caste characteristic still holds, and one evidence of it is that one is either black or not—partial degrees of blackness, despite the reality of a very mixed genetic inheritance, will not be recognized, not by our Census, not by our society. We do not recognize partial or loose affiliation with the group, or none at all, for blacks, as we do for all other ethnic and racial groups.

The racial categories the census uses to place each Asian group within its own special "race"—so that the Chinese, Japanese, Koreans, Asian Indians, and so on are each statistically a different "race"—is an anomaly and does not reflect the social reality that we recognize the children of white-Asian intermarriage as mixed, while we recognize the children of black-Asian intermarriage (or black-white intermarriage) as black. This is the reality that reflects the caste status of blacks in the American mind.

This is not to say that the caste is uniformly considered inferior. Even in the home of caste society, India, persons of lower castes rise to the highest positions, and caste somewhat weakens its hold over time, and this is true in the United States. This castelike character of American blacks will and must change, but it has not yet, and we do not know all the processes by which it will change, and what measures precisely will contribute to that change.

Insistence in our schools that we are all Americans and nothing less, that the changes that fully incorporate blacks have already occurred, that blacks are only Americans of darker skin, while true enough in law, is contradicted by reality. That contradiction has undermined the uniform education regarding our past and our culture that so many of us underwent and whose passing we lament. But it has passed, and we do not know, as our recent experiences with curricular change have shown, how it can be reconstructed. It seems we must pass through a period in which we recognize difference, we celebrate difference, we turn the spotlight on the inadequacies in the integration of our minorities in our past and present, and we raise up for special consideration the achievements of our minorities and their putative ancestors. All this is premised on our failure to integrate blacks. Others are included in this process; but it is the response to blacks, their different condition, their different perspective, that sets the model.

If I were writing in a normative mode—what is best, what do I prefer, what do I propose for America concerning its ethnic and racial diversity—I would say more or less what David Hollinger and others who respect the diversity of American origins but appreciate fully the power of the integrating values of our common society say: Let us have respect for identity in the context of a common culture, but let us avoid the fixing of lines of division on ethnic and racial bases. Let us accept the reality of exit from an ethnic-racial-religious group, as well as the right of differential attachment, as a common American way, and let us agree that ethnic and racial affiliation should be as voluntary as religious affiliation, and of as little concern to the state and public authority. Let us understand that more and more Americans want to be Americans simply, and nothing more, and let us celebrate that choice, and agree it would be better for America if more of us accepted that identity as our central one, as against ethnic and racial identities.

Hollinger's "postethnic perspective" favors "voluntary over involuntary affiliations, balances an appreciation for communities of descent with a determination to make room for new communities, and promotes solidarities of wide scope that incorporate people with different ethnic and racial backgrounds . . . [It] resists the grounding of knowledge and moral values in blood and history, but works within the last generation's recognition that many of the ideas and values once taken to be universal are specific to certain cultures."[8] I agree. My own list of preferences would be slightly different, with somewhat different nuances, but Hollinger's is good enough for our common society. But his prescription does not take account of the African American condition, where affiliation is hardly voluntary, where the community of descent defines an inescapable community of fate, where knowledge and moral values are indeed grounded in blood and history; one wonders how, or when, it will be otherwise.

"We are all multiculturalists now." Of course we are not *all* multiculturalists, but one would be hard put, if one works in schools and with black schoolchildren, so many of whom attend schools in which they make up all or a good part of the enrollment, to find someone who is not. The expression "We are all multiculturalists now" harks back to others that have been pronounced wryly by persons who recognized that something unpleasant was nevertheless unavoidable; it is not employed to indicate a wholehearted embrace. "We are all socialists now," Sir William Harcourt, Chancellor of the Exchequer in one of Gladstone's cabinets, was reputed to have said in 1889.[9] His best-known achievement was to get Parliament to accept progressive taxation on estates at death, a modest progressive tax at the time but one which outraged owners of the great estates. One assumes that Sir William did not mean socialism was the right thing, or the best thing, but simply that, if one considered progressive taxation on estates at death socialism, it was the inevitable thing, and one had to accept it. One could still argue about the details, as one can still argue about the details of just what kind of multiculturalism we should have.

The problems of divisiveness that multiculturalism raises at the level of the curriculum, or the school, or the culture, cannot be settled within the curriculum, the school, or the larger culture. The "culture wars" reflect many things, but when it comes to the division of blacks and others, they reflect a hard reality that none of us wants, that all of us want to see disappear, but that none of us knows how to overcome. It is only change in that larger reality that will reduce multiculturalism to a passing phase in the complex history of the making of an American nation from many strands.

NOTES

▲ ▲ ▲

1. The Multicultural Explosion

1. "School Board Will Recognize Other Cultures, but as Inferior," *New York Times*, May 13, 1994, Section A, p. 16.

2. Larry Rohter, "Battle over Patriotism Curriculum," *New York Times*, May 13, 1994, Section 1, p. 22.

3. "The 1994 Campaign: America First Policy Is Rejected," *New York Times*, October 7, 1994, Section A, p. 28.

4. Lynne V. Cheney, *Telling the Truth* (New York: Simon & Schuster, 1995), p. 31.

5. Todd Gitlin, *The Twilight of Common Dreams* (New York: Metropolitan Books, 1995), p. 41.

6. See, for example, Dinesh D'Souza, *Illiberal Education: The Politics of Race and Sex on Campus* (New York: The Free Press, 1991); Richard Bernstein, *Dictatorship of Virtue: Multiculturalism and the Battle for America's Future* (New York: Knopf, 1994); for counteraccounts of some of the incidents, see Russell Jacoby, *Dogmatic Wisdom: How the Culture Wars Divert Education and Distract America* (New York: Doubleday, 1994), ch. 2.

7. Catherine Cornbleth and Dexter Waugh, *The Great Speckled Bird: Multicultural Politics and Education Policymaking* (New York: St. Martin's Press, 1995), pp. 35–41 and elsewhere.

8. The quotation is from Mark Gerson, *The Neoconservative Vision* (Cambridge: Harvard University Press, 1996), and is quoted in a review by Peter Brooks, "Critics Will Be Losers," *The Times Literary Supplement*, August 30, 1996, p. 8.

9. Mark Gerson, *In the Classroom: Dispatches from an Inner-City School That Works* (New York: The Free Press, 1996).

10. See Robert Lerner, Althea K. Nagai, and Stanley Rothman, *Molding the Good Citizen* (Westport, Conn.: Praeger, 1995).

2. The New York Story

1. The story is told by David Kirp, "Textbooks and Tribalism in California," *The Public Interest,* 104 (Summer 1991): 20–36, and in greater detail in Todd Gitlin, *The Twilight of Common Dreams* (New York: Metropolitan Books, 1995), pp. 7–36, and in even fuller detail in Catherine Cornbleth and Dexter Waugh, *The Great Speckled Bird: Multicultural Politics and Educational Policymaking* (New York: St. Martin's Press, 1995), ch. 3.

2. See Nathan Glazer, "Levin, Jeffries, and the Fate of Academic Freedom," *The Public Interest,* 120 (Summer 1995): 14–40.

3. *A Curriculum of Inclusion,* Report of the Commissioner's Task Force on Minorities: Equity and Excellence (Albany: New York State Education Department, July 1989).

4. The statement was published in a number of places, among them the New York newspaper *Newsday,* June 29, 1990, p. A15, and that is the source from which I quote.

5. *One Nation, Many Peoples: A Declaration of Cultural Interdependence,* The Report of the New York State Social Studies Review and Development Committee (Albany: New York State Education Department, June 1991). Arthur Schlesinger's dissent presented in brief the thesis of his important book attacking multiculturalism, *The Disuniting of America: Reflections on a Multicultural Society* (New York: Norton, 1991).

6. "Who Are We? American Kids Are Getting a New—and Divisive—View of Thomas Jefferson, Thanksgiving, and the Fourth of July," and Paul Gray, "Whose America?" *Time,* July 8, 1991, pp. 12–17. "Mr. Sobol's Planet," *The New Republic,* July 15 and 22, 1991, pp. 5–7.

7. Joseph Berger, "Ethnic Studies Not New to Many Schools," *New York Times,* June 2, 1991, p. B1.

8. Joseph Berger, "McCall Says He Will Push for More Minority Teachers," *New York Times,* June 28, 1991, p. B1.

9. David Reich, "The S.A.T. Goes P.C.," *New York Times,* June 3, 1991.

10. Robert Lerner, Althea Nagai, and Stanley Rothman, "Gendering American History," *The World and I,* April 1996, pp. 336, 337. The sources are Diane Ravitch and Chester E. Finn, Jr., *What Do Our Seventeen-Year-Olds Know?* (New York: Harper & Row, 1987), pp. 8, 263–277; *U.S. News and World Report,* April 12, 1993, p. 63.

11. "Academia Retooling American Image," *Boston Globe,* June 30, 1991.

3. What Is at Stake in Multiculturalism?

1. *Multiculturalism and the Politics of Recognition* (Princeton: Princeton University Press, 1992).

2. On Afrocentrism, there is the admirable book by Mary Lefkowitz, *Not Out of Africa* (New York: Basic Books, 1996). The most substantial effort to place Africa, in the form of ancient Egypt, in a more central role in world history is Martin Bernal's *Black Athena: The Afrocentric Roots of Classical Civilization* (New Brunswick, N.J.: Rutgers University Press, 1987). For a critique, see Mary Lefkowitz and Guy Walter, eds., *Black Athena Revisited* (Chapel Hill, N.C.: University of North Carolina Press, 1996).

3. The fullest account of this pageant is to be found in Lawrence W. Levine, *The Opening of the American Mind* (Boston: Beacon Press, 1996), pp. 110–111.

4. Jennifer L. Hochschild, *Facing Up to the American Dream* (Princeton: Princeton University Press, 1995), p. 106.

5. Stanley Rothman, "Execution by Quota?" *The Public Interest,* 116 (Summer 1994).

6. Terrie Epstein, "Constructing Differences in African American and European American Adolescents' Perspectives on Significance in United States History: Implications for Curricular Reform," unpublished paper, July 1996.

7. For a summary of some of the research showing equal or higher self-esteem among blacks than among whites, and a critique of the theory that self-esteem is necessary for achievement, see Stephen P. Powers, David J. Rothman, and Stanley Rothman, "The Myth of Black Low Self-Esteem," *The World & I,* March 1990, pp. 563–581. For one example of a large-scale study demonstrating the existence of high black self-esteem, see John W. Osborne, "Academics, Self-Esteem, and Race: A Look at the Underlying Assumptions of the Disidentification Hypothesis," *Personality and Social Psychology Bulletin* 21, no. 5 (May 1995): 449–455.

8. Diane Ravitch and Chester E. Finn, Jr., *What Do Our Seventeen-Year-Olds Know?* (New York: Harper & Row, 1987), pp. 263–277.

9. Paul E. Peterson, Jay P. Grene, and Chad Noyes, "School Choice in Milwaukee," *The Public Interest,* 125 (Fall 1996): 38–56.

▲ ▲ ▲

4. The Rediscovery of Nubia and Kush

1. Catherine Cornbleth and Dexter Waugh, *The Great Specked Bird: Multicultural Politics and Education Policymaking* (New York: St. Martin's Press, 1995), pp. 12–13.

2. For a full account of this enterprise see Diane Ravitch, *National Standards in American Education: A Citizen's Guide* (Washington, D.C.: The Brookings Institution, 1995).

3. See Lynne V. Cheney's criticism in *Telling the Truth* (New York: Simon & Schuster, 1995), pp. 26–29. Harriet Tubman has by now achieved iconic status. To illustrate an article advocating national standards in education (Sara Mosle, "The Answer Is National Standards," *New York Times Magazine*, October 27, 1996, pp. 44 ff), the magazine reproduced on its cover some test questions one might expect to find if national standards become a reality. The only proper names to appear in the questions are those of Bill Clinton, Bob Dole, and Harriet Tubman.

4. For an account of the conflict over the standards, see Karen Diegmueller and Diane Viadero, "Playing Games with History," *Education Week*, November 25, 1995, pp. 29–34.

5. Lynne V. Cheney, "New History Standards Still Attack Our Heritage," *Wall Street Journal*, May 2, 1996.

6. John Patrick Diggins, "History Standards Get It Wrong Again," *New York Times*, May 15, 1996.

7. *National Standards for History: Basic Edition*, National Center for History in the Schools (Los Angeles: University of California, Los Angeles, 1996), pp. 77–78.

8. Ibid., p. 142.

9. Ibid., p. 143.

10. Ibid., p. 148.

11. How much is the new prominence of Nubia and Kush to be explained by political influences, how much by new archaeological findings or new evaluations of older findings? In the *New York Times* of February 11, 1992, John Noble Wilford takes account of the new prominence of Nubia and reports that both factors have played a role in bringing Nubia to greater attention: "Nubian Treasures Reflect Black Influence on Egypt," February 11, 1992, p. B1. Another article in the *New York Times* of the same date—Clyde Farnsworth, "Unlocking More Secrets of Nubian Civilization," p. B2—reports on new museum exhibits on

▲ ▲ ▲

Nubia, permanent and temporary. There is clearly much of great interest in ancient Nubian civilization, but it is also clear that one reason American museums are interested in mounting Nubian exhibits is because they hope such exhibits will appeal to African Americans.

12. *National Standards for History*, pp. 151–153.

13. Todd Gitlin emphasizes this factor in his excellent treatment of the fight over the history standards, in *The Twilight of Common Dreams* (New York: Metropolitan Books, 1995), pp. 189–199. He has corresponded with Morton Keller and Akira Iriye, who were among the historians in the National Council for History Standards, and their comments reflect the reality that history as a discipline has changed, and the standards reflect that change.

14. Karen Diegmueller, "N.Y. Regents OK Academic Standards, New School Regulations," *Education Week*, August 7, 1996.

15. *Learning Standards for the Social Studies*, rev. ed. (New York: New York State Education Department, June 1996).

5. Dealing with Diversity, Past and Present

1. Diane Ravitch, *The Great School Wars: New York City, 1805–1973* (New York: W. W. Norton: 1973).

2. David B. Tyack, *The One Best System: A History of American Urban Education* (Cambridge: Harvard University Press, 1974), p. 109.

3. Horace M. Kallen, "Democracy versus the Melting Pot," *The Nation*, February 18, 1915, pp. 190–192, and February 25, 1915, pp. 217–220; and Randolph Bourne, "Transnational America," *Atlantic*, 118 (July 1916): 86–97. The Kallen essay is reprinted in his *Culture and Democracy in the United States* (New York: Boni and Liveright, 1924). The Bourne essay is available in Randolph Bourne, *The History of a Literary Radical* (New York: S. A. Russell, 1956), and in other collections of his writings.

4. This passage from John Dewey can be found in Kallen, *Culture and Democracy*, pp. 131–132.

5. *Meyer* v. *State of Nebraska*, 262 U.S. 390 (1923); and *Pierce* v. *Society of Sisters*, 268 U.S. 510 (1925).

6. For a brief characterization of the movement, see Nathan Glazer, *Ethnic Dilemmas, 1964–1982* (Cambridge: Harvard University Press, 1983), pp. 102–107; for a fuller treatment, see Michael R. Olneck, "The

Recurring Dream: Symbolism and Ideology in Intercultural and Multicultural Education," *American Journal of Education* 97 (1989): 398–423.

6. Where Assimilation Failed

1. Crèvecoeur, *Letters from an American Farmer,* as quoted in Philip Gleason, "American Identity and Americanization," in *Harvard Encyclopedia of American Ethnic Groups* (Cambridge: Harvard University Press, 1980), p. 33.

2. Gleason, "American Identity," p. 31.

3. Nathan Glazer, *Affirmative Discrimination: Ethnic Inequality and Public Policy* (New York: Basic Books, 1975; Cambridge: Harvard University Press, 1987), ch. 5.

4. Gleason, "American Identity," p. 32.

5. Harold J. Abramson, "Assimilation and Pluralism," in *Harvard Encyclopedia of American Ethnic Groups,* p. 152.

6. John Higham, *Send These to Me: Immigrants in Urban America,* rev. ed. (Baltimore: Johns Hopkins University Press, 1984), p. 175.

7. Frances A. Kellor, "What Is Americanization?" *Yale Review,* January 1919, as reprinted in Philip Davis, *Immigration and Americanization: Selected Readings* (Boston: Ginn, 1920), pp. 625–626.

8. Davis, *Immigration and Americanization,* p. 612; for a description of the meeting, see Edward George Hartman, *The Movement to Americanize the Immigrant* (New York: AMS Press, 1967), p. 11, fn.

9. Davis, *Immigration and Americanization,* pp. 642–643.

10. Hartman, *The Movement to Americanize the Immigrant,* pp. 220–221.

11. James A. Gavit, *Americans by Choice* (New York: Harper, 1922), pp. 10, 11–12.

12. Ibid., pp. 7–8.

13. Frank V. Thompson, *Schooling of the Immigrant* (New York, Harper and Brothers, 1920), pp. 15–16.

14. Ibid., p. 16.

15. Ibid., p. 73.

16. Ibid., pp. 74, 118.

17. Nor can we find what was once a key sociological concept, "assimilation," among the entries in the recent four-volume *Encyclopedia of Sociology* by C. F. and M. L. Borgatta (New York: Macmillan, 1992).

▲ ▲ ▲

18. Read Lewis, "Americanization," *Encyclopedia of the Social Sciences* (New York: Macmillan, 1930), vol. 2, p. 33.

19. John Higham was perhaps the first to forcefully note the "fatal elision" of blacks from Horace Kallen's American orchestra of diverse ethnic and racial voices. See *Send These to Me,* 1st ed. (New York, Atheneum, 1975), p. 208.

20. See Chapter 5.

21. Horace Kallen, *Culture and Democracy in the United States* (New York: Boni and Liveright, 1924), pp. 127, 165.

22. For a characterization of the movement, see Nathan Glazer, *Ethnic Dilemmas, 1964–1982* (Cambridge: Harvard University Press, 1983), pp. 104–108.

23. Robert E. Park, "Assimilation," *Encyclopedia of the Social Sciences,* vol. 2, p. 282.

24. Louis Wirth, *The Ghetto* (Chicago: University of Chicago Press, 1928).

25. Gunnar Myrdal, *An American Dilemma* (New York: Harper, 1944)

26. See, for example, Brian Urquhart, *Ralph Bunche: An American Life* (New York: W. W. Norton, 1993), p. 57, and elsewhere for the position on this matter of a mainline black leader.

27. Lewis, "Americanization," p. 34.

28. Stanley Lieberson and Mary C. Waters, *From Many Strands: Ethnic and Racial Groups in Contemporary America* (New York: Russell Sage Foundation 1988), ch. 6.

29. Ibid., p. 45.

30. *Ethnic Options* (Berkeley: University of California Press, 1990).

31. Lieberson and Waters, *From Many Strands,* p. 182.

32. Douglas S. Massey and Nancy A. Denton, *American Apartheid: Segregation and the Making of the Underclass* (Cambridge: Harvard University Press, 1993).

7. Can We Be Brought Together?

1. Nathan Glazer, "On 'Opening Up' the Suburbs," *The Public Interest,* 37 (Fall 1974): 89–111. This article, in somewhat expanded form, became part of my book, *Affirmative Discrimination: Ethnic Inequality and Public Policy* (New York: Basic Books, 1975; Cambridge: Harvard University Press, 1987).

▲ ▲ ▲

2. Anthony Downs, *Opening Up the Suburbs: An Urban Strategy for America* (New Haven: Yale University Press, 1973).

3. Karl Taeuber and Alma Taeuber, *Negroes in Cities* (Chicago: Aldine, 1965).

4. Ben Wattenberg and R. M. Scammon, "Black Progress and Liberal Rhetoric," *Commentary*, 55 (1973): 35–44.

5. Irving Kristol, "The Negro Today Is Like the Immigrant Yesterday," *New York Times Magazine*, September 11, 1966.

6. Nathan Glazer and Daniel P. Moynihan, *Beyond the Melting Pot* (Cambridge: MIT Press, 1963).

7. Sam Lubell, *The Future of American Politics* (New York: Harper and Bros., 1952).

8. Gerald David Jaynes and Robin M. Williams, Jr., *A Common Destiny: Blacks and American Society* (Washington, D.C.: National Academy Press, 1989).

9. Richard Alba, *Ethnic Identity: The Transformation of White America* (New Haven: Yale University Press, 1990). Mary Waters, *Ethnic Options: Choosing Identities in America* (Berkeley: University of California Press, 1990).

10. Seymour Martin Lipset and Earl Raab, *Jews and the New American Scene* (Cambridge: Harvard University Press, 1995).

11. Ibid., pp. 183, 184. See too William Petersen, "Politics and the Measurement of Ethnicity," in William Alonso and Paul Starr, eds., *The Politics of Numbers* (New York: Russell Sage Foundation, 1987), p. 224, n. 75: "A study of Spanish-surnamed Californians found that between one third and two fifths married out, with little difference by age or sex." The study referred to is Robert Schoen, Verne E. Nelson, and Marion Collins, "Intermarriage among Spanish-Surnamed Californians, 1962–1974," *International Migration Review*, 12 (1978): 359–369.

12. Stanley Lieberson and Mary C. Waters, *From Many Strands: Ethnic and Racial Groups in Contemporary America* (New York: Russell Sage Foundation, 1988), p. 173.

13. Matthijs Kalmijn, "Trends in Black-White Intermarriage," *Social Forces*, 72 (1993): 119–146; and Douglas J. Besharov and Timothy S. Sullivan, "One Flesh: America Is Experiencing an Unprecedented Increase in Black-White Intermarriage," *The New Democrat*, July–August 1996, pp. 19–21.

14. Douglas S. Massey and Nancy A. Denton, *American Apartheid:*

Segregation and the Making of the Underclass (Cambridge: Harvard University Press, 1993).

15. Ibid., p. 63.

16. Ibid., pp. 32, 66, 67, 86, 91.

17. Thomas Schelling, "On the Ecology of Micromotives," *The Public Interest*, 25 (Fall 1971): 59–98.

18. For example, Jon Rieder, *Canarsie* (Cambridge: Harvard University Press, 1985).

19. Richard P. Taub, D. Garth Taylor, and Jan D. Dunham, *Paths of Neighborhood Change: Race and Crime in Urban America* (Chicago: University of Chicago Press, 1984), pp. 113–118, 135, 136.

20. David M. Cutler and Edward L. L. Glaeser, "Are Ghettoes Good or Bad?" Harvard University and National Bureau for Economic Research, unpublished paper, 1995.

21. William Labov and Wendell A. Harris, "De Facto Segregation of Black and White Vernaculars," in David Sankoff, ed., *Diversity and Diachrony* (Amsterdam and Philadelphia: John Benjamins, 1986), pp. 17–18.

22. Paul Farhi, "A Television Trend: Audiences in Black and White," *Washington Post*, November 29, 1994.

23. Massey and Denton, *American Apartheid*, p. 63.

24. Ibid., pp. 63, 64, 65.

25. Jennifer L. Hochschild, *Facing Up to the American Dream* (Princeton: Princeton University Press, 1995), p. 152.

26. See David L. Kirp, John P. Dwyer, and Larry A. Rosenthal, *Our Town: Race, Housing, and the Soul of Suburbia* (New Brunswick, N.J.: Rutgers University Press, 1995); and Charles M. Haar, *Suburbs under Siege* (Princeton: Princeton University Press, 1996).

27. Harold Husock, "Subsidizing Discrimination at Starrett City," *City Journal*, 2, no. 1 (1992): 48–53.

28. Hillel Levine and Lawrence Harmon, *The Death of an American Jewish Community: A Tragedy of Good Intentions* (New York: Free Press, 1992).

29. Taub et al., *Paths of Neighborhood Change*.

30. Andrew Wiese, "Neighborhood Diversity: Social Change, Ambiguity, and Fair Housing," *Journal of Urban Affairs*, 17 (1995): 107–130.

31. J. Rosenbaum et al., "Can the Kerner Commission's Housing Strategy Improve Employment, Education, and Social Integration for Low-Income Blacks?" *North Carolina Law Review*, 71 (1993): 1519–1556;

Leonard S. Rubinowitz, "Metropolitan Public Housing Desegregation Remedies: Chicago's Privatization Program," *Northern Illinois University Law Review,* 12 (1992): 589–669.

32. Downs, *Opening Up the Suburbs,* ch. 12.

33. Harold Husock, "A Critique of Mixed Income Housing," *The Responsive Community,* 5 no. 2 (1995): 34–49.

34. Glenn Loury, *One by One: From the Inside Out* (New York: Free Press, 1995).

8. "We Are All Multiculturalists Now"

1. Todd Gitlin, *The Twilight of Common Dreams* (New York: Metropolitan Books, 1995), p. 227. He is certainly aware that all these groups are of different weight and consequence, and a page later writes: "Yet in many ways, the jargon of multiculturalism, whether as angel or bogeyman, evades the central wound in American history. America's national history . . . is thick with slaughter and misery, and none of the consequences are more biting, more disturbing, than today's conflicts between whites and blacks." But he hurries past this in his concern for his central point, the need to construct a new alliance of the left transcending race, ethnicity, sex, and other bases for identity claims.

2. The "two nations" quotation is from Disraeli's *Sybil,* as quoted in Mark Gerson, *In the Classroom: Dispatches from an Inner-City School That Works* (New York: Free Press, 1996), p. 203.

3. Andrew Hacker, *Two Nations: Black and White, Separate, Hostile, Unequal* (New York: Scribner, 1992). For Gerson *(In the Classroom)* too the "two nations" are more the black and white than the rich and poor.

4. Reed Ueda, "Naturalization and Citizenship," *Harvard Encyclopedia of American Ethnic Groups* (Cambridge: Harvard University Press, 1980), p. 748.

5. Nathan Glazer, *Affirmative Discrimination: Ethnic Inequality and Public Policy* (New York: Basic Books, 1975; Cambridge: Harvard University Press, 1987).

6. Ronald Takaki, "Reflections on Racial Patterns in America," in Takaki, ed., *From Different Shores* (New York: Oxford University Press, 1987), pp. 26–37.

7. *Charting a Course: Social Studies for the 21st Century,* Report of the

Curriculum Task Force of the National Commission on Social Studies in the Schools, 1989, p. 1.

8. David A. Hollinger, *Postethnic America* (New York: Basic Books, 1995), p. 3.

9. It may be apocryphal. The source is Hubert Bland, in George Bernard Shaw et al., *Fabian Essays* (London: George Allen and Unwin, 1962; 1st ed., 1889), p. 244.

ACKNOWLEDGMENTS

▲ ▲ ▲

A good part of Chapters 2, 4, and 5 appeared in an earlier version in a paper published under the title "Multiculturalism and Public Policy" in *Values and Public Policy*, edited by Henry J. Aaron, Thomas E. Mann, and Timothy Taylor (Washington, D.C.: Brookings Institution, 1994). An earlier version of Chapter 3 appeared under the title "Five Questions about Multiculturalism," in *Can Democracy Be Taught?* edited by Andrew Oldenquist (Bloomington, Ind.: Phi Delta Kappa Foundation, 1996). An earlier version of Chapter 6 was originally presented in 1993 as a paper to the Symposium on Science, Reason, and Modern Democracy, Michigan State University, and was published in *The Annals*, vol. 530 (November 1993), under the title, "Is Assimilation Dead?" Chapter 7 originally appeared in *The Public Interest*, Summer 1995, under the title "Black and White after Thirty Years." All have been reworked and revised and updated for this book.

I was able to spend a month at the Bellagio Center of the Rockefeller Foundation to work on the materials that have become this book, and I would like to express my appreciation to the Foundation. Susan Wallace Boehmer of Harvard University Press and my wife, Sulochana Raghavan Glazer, read the manuscript closely a number of times and made particularly helpful suggestions and corrections. I am grateful to them.

INDEX

▲ ▲ ▲

▲ ▲ ▲